READINGS IN LONG ISLAND ARCHAEOLOGY and ETHNOHISTORY

Volume I

Early Papers in Long Island Archaeology

Introduction
Dr. Bert Salwen

Foreword
Gaynell S. Levine

Preface
Ben Werner, Jr.

This customized Reader has been published as part of the
XEROX INDIVIDUALIZED PUBLISHING PROGRAM.

Harrington articles reprinted with the permission of the American Museum of Natural History.

Ferguson, Orchard, and Saville articles reprinted with permission and in cooperation with the Museum of the American Indian: Heye Foundation.

CONTENTS

WHY THE SUFFOLK COUNTY ARCHAEOLOGICAL ASSOCIATION?

An agency is needed to–

*promote the conservation of cultural resources sites for scientific study, excavation and preservation as places of historical significance

*develop a program of public education for a more responsible attitude toward cultural resources

*provide opportunity for interested individuals and groups to play a meaningful role in local scientific research

*seek the support of local agencies and governmental institutions to preserve our cultural remains before it is too late

S.C.A.A. OFFICERS and BOARD MEMBERS

This volume would not have been possible without the vision and support of **RUFUS LANGHANS,** *Huntington Town Historian,* and is affectionately dedicated to his creative expression of that role.

This publication has been made possible, in part, by a grant from the *Long Island Lighting Company.*

Preface

This volume has been designed as an introduction to the early archaeological work done on and around Long Island, New York. It will be useful for serious students of archaeology, for historians, and for laymen interested in the field.

For almost a century a variety of individuals have been researching the early Indian and Colonial past of Coastal New York. To date, much of the written data has been unpublished or lost in the files of archaeological societies, historical societies, museums, newspapers, and magazines. Much of this information has been extremely difficult to locate, as by now the early materials are either completely unavailable or long out of print. This dearth of original materials has greatly complicated the learning, teaching and researching of the early cultural complexes of Long Island and the surrounding regions.

The articles in the volume are presented "in situ" with the understanding that, with the passage of time, ideas, techniques, concepts, and theories have been altered by recent research. The reader is urged to keep this in mind while using the work.

This volume is, we hope, the first of several which will provide the opportunity for all interested parties to read the thoughts and data of early researchers into Long Island prehistory and history.

BEN WERNER, JR., President
Suffolk County Archaeological Association

Acknowledgements

Many people have contributed ideas and support for the birth of this reprint series. We are grateful to the staffs of the American Museum of Natural History; the Museum of the American Indian, especially Alexander Draper's constructive assistance; the Nassau County Museum System– Garvies Point Museum & Preserve; SUNY at Stony Brook Library. Also Dorothy King, Curator of the Long Island Collection, East Hampton Free Library, Eleanor Lundin, Margaret Sepenoski, Jeanne Vinicombe, Dick Solo, Virginia Merola, and Mary Mallery participated in producing this volume.

Notable assistance was also given by the continuing support of Dr. Phil Weigand and Dr. Margaret Wheeler, the counsel of Dr. Dolores Newton, and the suggestion for format by Dr. W. Arens, all of the Anthropology Department, State University of New York at Stony Brook.

Dr. Lynn Ceci, Queens College, sparked the idea of a reprint series by her lecture, "Problems of Long Island Archaeology," given for Dr. Weigand's Continuing Education Department course, *Introduction to Long Island Archaeology,* SUNY, Stony Brook, Spring, 1975.

Dr. Bert Salwen of New York University, dean of area coastal archaeologists, deserves our heartiest appreciation for undertaking his commentary during a year of exceptionally heavy professional commitments.

FOREWORD

The rapid Eastward urban development of Long Island has hastened the destruction of the area's prehistoric and historic archaeological remains– our irreplaceable cultural resources– and many other factors have combined on Long Island to foster one of the highest destruction rates in the nation.

Rising coastal water levels have inundated the earliest prehistoric habitation sites, as demonstrated by Dr. Salwen's research, and the acidic soil is deleterious to the artifactual evidence of life. A proliferation of 'pot-hunters', those who dig for their own pleasure and collections, has destroyed much of the scientific record forever.

Among the earliest areas of North America affected by European contact and colonization, Long Island's sites and aboriginal inhabitants were among the first to be affected. Unfortunately, few early explorers or missionaries spent extended periods of time or extensively recorded the area to provide the "early ethnography" that exists for some areas of the country. Again, with the birth of American anthropology at the turn of the century, ethnographic attention was rarely directed toward Long Island's few remaining aboriginal inhabitants. The few Metropolitan-area trained anthropologists of that era usually departed for other areas of the country. State government-level scientists far removed by geography and by interest have contributed to little professional interest in what has been considered a "backwater" area, in aboriginal culture terms.

It has been said that, after Thomas Jefferson's strata-by-strata excavation of an Indian burial mound near his home in 1782, the next scientific, or stratified, excavation in the country was by Harrington on Long Island at the turn of the last century. Harrington excavated on Long Island while an Assistant in Anthropology for the American Museum of Natural History, and published much of this research while working for the Museum of the American Indian: Heye Foundation for varying periods between 1908-28.

Not only is the early ethnographic and archaeological record relatively sparse, but what has been recorded and excavated is in large part not on Long Island, but scattered in museums throughout the country or in private collections. Until recently, only two doctorates (focusing on "coastal archaeology") had been awarded to Carlyle Smith and Bert Salwen; future Long Island studies will benefit from the more recent research of Lorraine Williams, Rose Oldfield Hayes, and Lynn Ceci.

The early archaeology reported in this volume occurred when many archaeologists were still discarding pottery sherds that were not decorative or faunal or vegetal remains indicating seasonal usage, which were not demed to be of interest at that time, but which are carefully preserved and avalyzed today. There was little or no interest or support for North American archaeology at that time and few trained people, as will be evident in the **Biographical Data** section.

Now that we know that the unique siting of Mesa Verde pueblo inside an overhanging rock shelter was done for climate control purposes, we should be newly aware of our predecessors' ability to live in partnership with nature. The aboriginal inhabitants maintained a balanced eco-system which we can learn from in these energy-conscious times.

Archaeology is the only science whose investigations destroy the object of its inquiry, so excavation should be conducted only by trained personnel with adequate institutional backing to assure careful excavation, analysis, and publication. Many new diagnostic techniques– Carbon14; geomorphology; pollen analysis; soil Ph, phosphates, and resistivity testing; neutron activation and spectrographic analysis; thermoluminescence and archaeomagnetic dating; water flotation techniques, etc.– have been developed for more accurate dating, identification, and analysis; with the exception of C14, their use in Long Island archaeology is just beginning.

Scientific archaeology includes careful excavation, cleaning, cataloging, preservation treatment if necessary, safe storage, publication of the site report, and interpretation for the public. Most of the results of excavation by avocational archaeologists on Long Island has not been written up or published, nor have scientific diagnostic techniques been utilized, so much of the scientific record has been lost. No professional archaeologist buys, trades, or sells artifacts, nor are burial grounds knowingly excavated today. Archaeological sites have no protection beyond the owner's concern, as no antiquities laws for other than State-owned sites exist and the State has not been enforcing its own regulations on Long Island, particularly regarding marine archaeology.

Due to the number of known sites today, the large number of unknown sites, and development pressures necessitating urgent salvage archaeology projects, today the archaeological profession is urging identification and preservation of sites, not necessarily immediate excavation. Excavation should be undertaken only if the site is endangered or if some cogent theoretical problem may be clarified by such site findings. During excavation, only a portion of the site should be excavated, leaving the balance for the inevitably more sophisticated techniques and theories of the future. Hopefully, future archaeology on Long Island will utilize model-testing, problem-oriented research design, as is now being done in other parts of the country.

So little is known of the extent of cultural remains on Eastern Long Island that S.C.A.A. was awarded a grant this year from the New York State Council on the Arts, Architecture and Environmental Arts Section, to compile a Cultural Resources Inventory. A publication outlining the results of the project will be placed in local libraries and agencies and the Inventory itself in appropriate government agencies. Hopefully, a further grant will be secured to develop a predictive model for site location; this will be an extremely useful tool for planning and land management agencies in future.

The organization of the Nassau Archaeological Society in the 1950s led to the utilization of professional advice from Irving Rouse of Yale University and State Archaeologist William Ritchie for excavations in Nassau County; to the publication of findings in N.A.S. Bulletin No. 1, 1955; and eventually, through the leadership of Edward Patterson, to the development of the archaeological and geological branch of the Nassau County Museum System, the Garvies Point Museum & Preserve, staffed by professional personnel. Suffolk County, the only remaining archaeologically-viable area on Long Island, has no county archaeologist or county-supported natural history/science museum to foster a concern for our unseen cultural remains– prehistoric and Colonial, to manage or preserve these resources, or to interpret our cultural heritage for local residents or interested visitors.

It has often been said that we do not know who we are if we do not know from whence we came. In that vein, S.C.A.A. has undertaken the reprinting of early Long Island records, documents, histories, and reports so that we may have access to our past cultural record.

GAYNELL S. LEVINE, Corresponding Secretary
Suffolk County Archaeological Society
Readings Series Editor

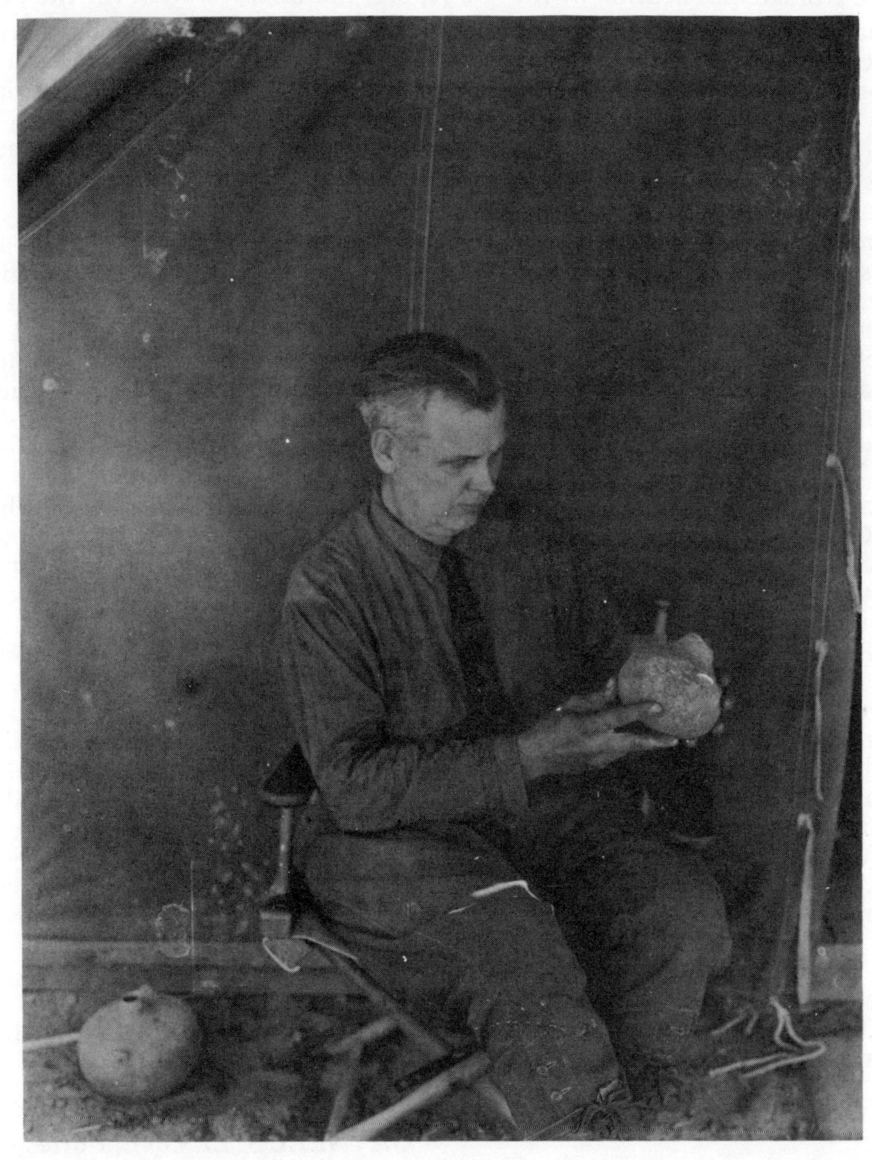

Mark Raymond Harrington

Photograph courtesy of the Museum of the American Indian: Heye Foundation

BIOGRAPHICAL DATA

Mark Raymond Harrington, 1882-1971

M.R. Harrington cut his "archaeological teeth" on the Metropolitan-area sites (Anthropological Papers, American Museum of Natural History, Vol. 3, 1909, etc.) and Long Island sites reprinted here. He continued to become one of America's most noted anthropologists, equally versed in field collection, archaeology, and ethnology.

As a high school student he worked as an Anthropological Assistant at the American Museum of Natural History, 1899-1903, with the noted anthropologist of that day, Dr. Frederick W. Putnam, and as a summer field worker for the Peabody Museum, 1903-4. After two years at the University of Michigan, he completed a B.A. and M.A. at Columbia University under the leading anthropological figures, Adolph Bandelier and Franz Boas.

When a job at the American Museum of Natural History did not materialize, Harrington worked for Covert's Indian Store in New York City during 1907 as a field collector. A good part of his life was spent as an ethnographer and collector of fast-disappearing artifacts for the Museum of the American Indian: Heye Foundation in 1908-11, 1915-17, and 1919-28, as well as publishing the results of excavation in New York, New Jersey, Arkansas, Tennessee, the Midwest, Cuba, etc. He did not simply 'acquire' Indian material culture, but developed life-long friendships and a deep ethnographic knowledge of 43 Indian groups. He also worked for the University of Pennsylvania Museum, Carnegie Institute of Washington, and the National Park Service at various times.

Harrington joined the Southwest Museum in Los Angeles in 1928 and remained as Curator until 1964. He excavated and reported on Lovelock and Gypsum Caves, and Tule Spring, Nevada, and Borax Lake and other notable sites in California, which yielded some of the earliest dated remains of man in the West. Restoration of several Spanish missions and an ancient adobe house was among his contributions to California history.

Literally excavating his way across the country– Northeast to Southeast to Midwest to West– Harrington published over 325 works, many now in reprint; a large number of unpublished field observations were presented to the Museum of the American Indian, available for the use of all qualified scholars.

There is comparatively little information on the early archaeologists Henry Lee Ferguson, Frederick Preston Orchard, and Foster H. Saville, who excavated on Long Island and Fisher's Island early in the twentieth century. Their papers reprinted here represent the only published material for that time besides Harrington's. Ferguson appears to have excavated on Fisher's Island through a lifetime spent there; Orchard and Saville seem to have become involved through kinship with active archaeologists of the day, and their 'training' consisted of association, an apprenticeship, with practicing archaeologists of the day.

Henry Ferguson's father and uncle purchased a large part of Fisher's Island in 1889, when he was 7 years old. He and a friend, Blair Williams, became trustees of the Museum of the American Indian: Heye Foundation in the early 1930s, and it is probably because of that association that any of Ferguson's extensive explorations of Fisher's Island were written and printed. He died in 1959, an example of the 'gentleman' archaeologist of that period.

Frederick Orchard was the son of the well-known early ethnographer, William Orchard, who worked for the American Museum of Natural History before 1920 as a preparator and model maker, and had written papers on beadwork and quillwork of the American Indians. Frederick was a member of the Museum of the American Indian: Heye Foundation staff in the late 1920s and early 1930s, and may have worked for the Peabody Museum after leaving New York. He subsequently wrote "Indian Remains on Long Island," *El Palacio,* 1927, Vol. 23; "A Preliminary Bibliography of the Archaeology of the New England Indians," with Donald F. Brown, Massachusetts Archaeological Society

Bulletin, 1941, Vol. 3, No.1; and "A Standard System for Classification and Description of Stone Implements from New England," Massachusetts Archaeological Society *Bulletin*, 1941, Vol. 2, No. 3.

Foster Saville was the brother of the noted bibliophile and South and Central American archaeologist of early 1900s, Marshall Saville. He accompanied Marshall on expeditions to Ecuador and Southern Mexico for the Museum of the American Indian: Heye Foundation, and was known as an expert at cataloguing and preparing archaeological collections while on the Museum staff in the early 1920s. He subsequently was Curator of the Sandy Bay Historical Society Museum of Rockport, Mass., and proprietor of the Cape Ann Old Book Shop. He authored, with Roger Babson, "Cape Ann, An Historical Guide," and wrote for the Museum of the American Indian: Heye Foundation *Indian Notes,* "An Unusual Skull from Rhode Island," 1924, Vol. 1, and "Indian Wells on Long Island," 1924-5, Vol. 1-2, as well as the papers reprinted here. He died in 1942, aged 67.

EARLY PAPERS IN LONG ISLAND ARCHAEOLOGY

Introduction

When one examines the beginnings of the scientific study of prehistory in the coastal New York region, the work of two individuals, Alanson Skinner and Mark Raymond Harrington, stands almost alone. In the early years of their careers each was affiliated at different times with the American Museum of Natural History and the Museum of the American Indian: Heye Foundation. During the first 20 years of this century both archaeologists excavated extensively, and published the results of these excavations in a manner wholly consistent with the professional standards of the times. Skinner worked mainly on Staten Island, and he is therefore not represented in this collection of early papers on Long Island archaeology. Harrington's activities encompassed Long Island, and his report of excavations on the Island's south fork (Harrington 1924) is a major paper in this volume.

When, in the early 1920's, both moved on to other anthropological interests– Harrington to archaeology in the western United States and Skinner to the ethnography of the Great Plains– planned archaeological research in this area virtually ceased. Some amateurs and semiprofessionals continued to dig, but few publications, and even fewer scientifically useful ones, resulted from these efforts. Real progress did not resume until 1938, when Carlyle Smith and Ralph Solecki, two young Long Islanders with deep interest in the past of their home community, began to pool data and ideas.

This collaboration continued into graduate school at Columbia, where Smith wrote a doctoral dissertation, *The Archaeology of Coastal New York* (1950), that still provides the basic framework for prehistoric research in the region, and Solecki completed a master's thesis, *The Archaeological Position of Historic Fort Corchaug . . .* (also 1950), that set the contact period archaeology of Long Island on a firm foundation. I understand that the Suffolk County Archaeological Association plans to treat the work of these two researchers in later volumes in this series.

In this volume, six earlier papers are reprinted which represent, essentially, the "state of the art" at the time that Smith and Solecki began their research. Except for some very short reports (e.g., Parker 1922), a few unpublished manuscripts, and the specimen collections in local museums, this is literally all there was. Viewed in this context, these early papers, though they often seem frustratingly incomplete to today's scholars, assume their rightful importance.

The earliest paper in this collection is Harrington's (1909) general discussion of shell "heaps" in the New York Metropolitan area. Port Washington, Dosoris Pond, and Shinnecock Hills are among the Long Island areas discussed. The presentation is largely object-oriented, and Harrington is uncritical (or unaware) of the extent to which local collectors' digging was destroying information about the aboriginal past. Except for occasional references to "archaic-looking arrow points" or "very crude pottery" (1909:176), and the use of the now-outmoded bipartite division of ceramics into Algonkin and Iroquoian classes (1909:174), the paper reflects little of our present-day concern with culture history and culture change. Nevertheless, there is much in this short document that demonstrates its author's pioneering interest in some very "modern" problems. Note, for example, the discussion of the environmental factors in site selection (1909:169), the interest in food remains, other non-artifactual refuse, and "fire-broken stones" (1909:169-70), and the recognition of the importance of wear patterns on utilized stone flakes (1909:171). Finally, Harrington's carefully drawn stratigraphic profiles and his recognition that "shell heaps are often divided into layers, the deepest of which are of course, the oldest" (1909:170), may put our region into the running in the "earliest stratigraphic excavation" sweepstakes.

In 1917 and 1918, Foster Saville, a member of George Heye's staff at the Museum of the American Indian, excavated all that remained of the Montauk Indian cemetery at Pantigo, near Amagansett. His report (Saville 1920) clearly demonstrates the enormous importance of this site to our understanding of the Indian-European contact period on Long Island. By 1920s standards, the paper is quite complete. It contains a small site map, descriptions of each of the 39 burials excavated by the museum party (another 17 were removed by the property owner during the construction of a chicken house), and lists of the objects found with each burial as well as some information about the placement of these objects in relation to each other. The archaeologist who consults this report in search of data for the solution of contemporary problems will frequently be disappointed by the lack of plans and profiles and by the vagueness of many of the descriptions (e.g., "arrow-points . . . of white quartz and of the type usually found on Long Island"), but he must remember that Saville was writing for a very different reader. Smith (1950:159-60) was able to use some of Savilles' findings in his characterization of the Shantok tradition. Perhaps the republication of this paper will inspire some modern researcher to restudy the materials from Pantigo, still housed at the Museum of the American Indian, and to publish them in as much detail as their importance deserves.

As noted above, some of the earliest professional excavations on Long Island were conducted by Harrington in the very first years of the 20th century. In 1902, he dug extensively at a site on Sebonac Creek in the Shinnecock Hills region. His field crew consisted of Alanson Skinner, who was on his first dig, and Arthur C. Parker, later to become New York State Archaeologist, who was on his second! The report of this work, which was not published until 22 years later (Harrington 1924), reveals both the strengths and weaknesses inherent in Harrington's approach to archaeology. On the positive side, there is the sensitivity to stratigraphic indices which was noted earlier. He dug "test holes" and excavated by carefully trowelling down the exposed face of the cut (1924:235). He recognized boundaries between the "village layer" and the cooking and refuse pits which were only faintly indicated by "slight stains and bits of charcoal running down" into the sandy subsoil below the midden (1924:235). He was even able to isolate two "wigwam sites" (house floors?) (1924:238). There was also the interest in food remains and other non-artifactual specimens, and in the total culture of the occupants of the site.

Unfortunately, Harrington, like his contemporaries, did not think it necessary to fully describe the results of his acute field observations, and the report provides relatively little detailed description of specimens or information about proveniences. He also shared a belief widely held by his early 20th century colleagues that the Shinnecock, like all eastern Indians, "had not been located in eastern Long Island more than a few hundred years before the coming of the whites" (1924:283). Skinner had made the same assumption about the Lenape of Staten Island (1909:38). Hence, his "reconstruction of Shinnecock culture" is based on a free mixture of archaeological data with "information gathered from the descendants of this people, old local records, the writings of early travelers, and the surviving practices of similar tribes . . ." (Harrington 1924:246). This unsupported recourse to ethnographic analogy would be suspect today. In this particular case, we now know that the basic assumption was at least partially in error. When Smith reexamined the Sebonac collection at the American Museum of Natural History during his dissertation research, he discovered ceramic evidence for a series of occupations at the site (Smith 1950: 133-34, 180-81). He concluded that the major (Sebonac focus) occupation could not be clearly correlated with the historic Shinnecock (1950:181).

The three remaining papers in this volume have been reprinted primarily because they may provide comparative material for students engaged in distributional studies. Saville's (1926) brief description of two blade caches is the first documentation for this kind of fearture on Long Island. Comparison of this 5-page paper with the recently published analysis by Kaplan and Mills (1976) of a somewhat similar feature at Massapequa Lake dramatically points up the changes that have taken place in both the orientation and the technical facility of regional archaeologists.

Orchard's (1928) report on a salvage effort by the Museum of the American Indian in the Port Washington area is too short and incomplete to do justice to the excavated materials, but even so, the brief descriptions and photographs of some of the ceramic specimens support Smith's (1950: 171-72) characterization of the site as a component of the East River tradition, and– as in all cases where the site has been destroyed – this is all we have left.

The final paper (Ferguson 1935) reports on some 23 years of amateur activity on Fishers Island. From 1912 until 1929, efforts were limited to surface collecting, and the paper supplies some useful information about find spots for different classes of implements. After 1929, attention shifted to the excavation of shell middens. These are perfunctorily reported, as might be expected from the author's admission that "proper records have not been kept" (1935:xiii). The paper is included in this collection because, except for a brief reference by Ritchie (1959:88, P1.52), it contains the only published information about this Long Island outpost. Though printed in 1935, it fails to reflect any of the progressive changes in archaeological research since Harrington's 1909 effort. One can only hope that any remaining midden sites on the island will receive more informed attention. We can no longer afford this kind of conspicuous consumption of scarce and non-renewable resources.

References Cited

Ferguson, Henry L.
1935 **Archaeological Exploration of Fishers Island, New York.** Museum of the American Indian: Heye Foundation, *Indian Notes and Monographs*, Vol. 11, No. 1. New York.

Harrington, Mark Raymond
1909 **Ancient Shell Heaps Near New York City.** American Museum of Natural History, *Anthropological Papers*, Vol. 3, pp. 167-79. New York.
1924 **An Ancient Village Site of the Shinnecock Indians.** American Museum of Natural History, *Anthropological Papers*, Vol. 22, Pt. 5. New York.

Kaplan, Daniel H. and Herbert C. Mills
1976 **The Massapequa Lake Blade Cache.** New York State Archaeological Association, *Bulletin*, No. 66, pp. 18-31. Ann Arbor.

Orchard, F. P.
1928 **A Matinecoc Site on Long Island.** Museum of the American Indian: Heye Foundation, *Indian Notes*, Vol. 5, pp. 217-31. New York.

Parker, Arthur C.
1922 **The Archaeological History of New York. Parts 1-2.** New York State Museum, *Bulletin*, Nos. 235-36, 237-38. Albany.

Ritchie, William A.
1959 **The Stony Brook Site and its Relation to Archaic and Transitional Cultures on Long Island.** New York State Museum and Science Service, *Bulletin*, No. 372. Albany.

Saville, Foster H.
1920 **A Montauk Cemetery at Easthampton, Long Island.** Museum of the American Indian: Heye Foundation, *Indian Notes and Monographs*, Vol. 2, No. 3. New York.
1926 **Cache of Blades from Long Island.**Museum of the American Indian: Heye Foudnation, *Indian Notes*, Vol. 3, No. 1, pp. 41-45. New York.

Skinner, Alanson
1909 **The Lenape Indians of Staten Island.** American Museum of Natural History, *Anthropological Papers*, Vol. 3, pp. 3-62. New York.

Smith, Carlyle S.
1950 **The Archaeology of Coastal New York.** American Museum of Natural History, *Anthropological Papers*, Vol. 43, Pt. 2, New York.

Solecki, Ralph S.
1950 **The Archaeological Position of Historic Fort Corchaug, L.I., and its Relation to Contemporary Forts.** Archaeological Society of Connecticut, *Bulletin*, No. 24, pp. 3-40. New Haven.

Bert Salwen
Department of Anthropology
New York University
New York, New York

April, 1977

ANCIENT SHELL HEAPS NEAR NEW YORK CITY.

BY

M. R. HARRINGTON.

Of all the traces left by the aborigines along the New York seacoast, the most abundant and familiar are the shell heaps — the beds of refuse marking the sites of ancient villages, camps and isolated wigwams. Wherever the fresh water joins the salt and especially where open water for fishing, a creek with its clam beds, and a spring for drinking come together in happy combination, there is generally to be found some such evidence of Indian occupation, unless, as is often the case, settlement and improvement have buried deep the shells or carted them away.

The typical shell heap is not a "heap" at all, for leaf mold, the wash from neighboring high ground and often cultivation have made it level with its surroundings (Fig. 27). Very often, unless the land be plowed, no shells whatever show on the surface, and the only way of finding out the conditions

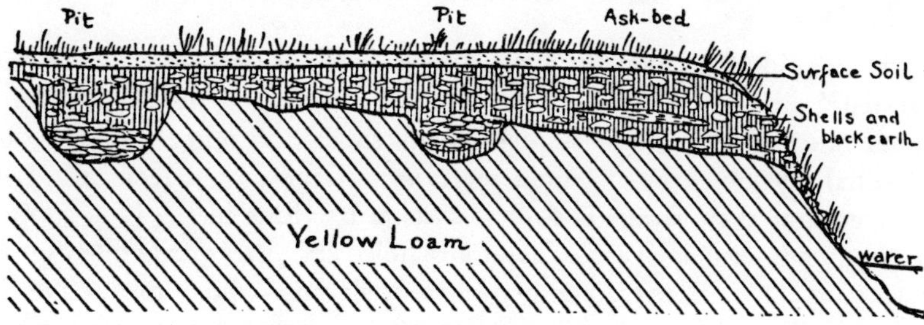

Fig. 27. Diagram of a Typical Shell Deposit.

of things below the sod is to test with a spade or a crowbar. If shells are present, their crunching soon gives notice of the fact. Sometimes shell heaps have been located by shells thrown from mole and woodchuck burrows, or by outcropping in gullies washed by the rain, or banks broken down by the surf. They are generally located near some creek or bay on low but dry ground, preferably with an eastern or southern exposure, and, as before mentioned not far from drinking water. Some have been found fronting on the open Sound, but such cases are rare. These deposits consist of large quantities of decayed oyster, clam, and other marine shells mixed with stained earth, with here and there ashes, charcoal and fire-broken stones to mark the spots where ancient camp fires blazed. Among the shells are usually scattered antler of deer, fish bones, bones of animals and birds split for the marrow, quantities of pottery fragments, and broken implements, in short, the imperishable part of the camp refuse left by the Indians. Now and then, perfect implements and ornaments that had been carelessly lost in the rubbish or hidden for safe-keeping are discovered. Little did the Indian think, as he laid away his little hoard, that his handiwork would never see light again until he and his people had long been gone and forgotten.

Shell heaps vary from a few inches to four feet in depth, and in area from a few square yards to several acres — all depending on the length of time the settlement was occupied and the number of dwellings comprising it.

Reprinted from American Museum of Natural History
ANTHROPOLOGICAL PAPERS, Vol. 3, 1909.

Deep shell heaps are often divided into layers, the deepest of which are, of

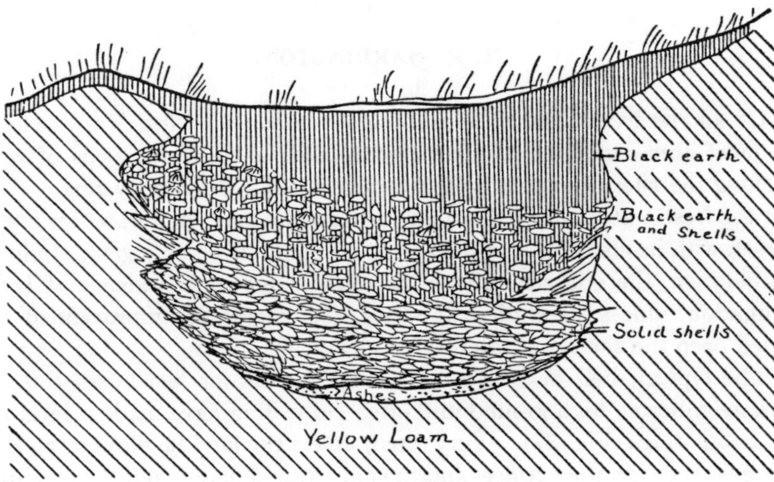

Fig. 28. Cross Section of a Shell Pit.

course, the oldest. Under and near most of these deposits may be found scattered "pits" or fire holes, which are bowl-shaped depressions in the ground filled with layers of stained earth, shells and other refuse, with an occasional layer of ashes. Some pits are as large as ten feet wide by six feet deep, but the average is four feet deep by three feet. It is supposed that they were used as ovens or steaming holes and afterwards filled up with refuse (Fig. 28). Some contain human skeletons, which may have been interred in them during the winter season when grave digging was impossible. Pits as a rule, contain more of interest than the ordinary shell layer. The closely packed regular masses of shells form a covering which tends to preserve bone implements, charred corn, and such perishable articles from decay, in a way that the looser shells of the general layers fail to do.

The implements, utensils and ornaments found in the shell heaps include objects made of stone, copper, bone and antler, shell and baked clay. Arrow points are among the most abundant of stone relics and exist in great variety, while larger points evidently intended for knives or spears are not uncommon. Drills are rare, but some very fine narrow blades of this class have been secured. Implements of stone called scrapers, with chipped beveled edges were probably used for scraping down arrow shafts or for scraping skin and the like, as a piece of glass is used by modern woodworkers. Sometimes mere flakes of stone show signs of use as knives or scrapers. Even more abundant than the arrow-heads themselves may be found rejects — the failures of arrow point making — stones that proved too obdurate to work, that broke, or that flaked improperly. Quartz was the favorite material for chipped implements in Westchester County and Long Island, probably because it might be found on any beach, while chert and jasper were harder to get, and argillite had to be imported from what is now New Jersey. This was frequently done, however, for greatly weathered argillite blades and fragments are often found in the local shell heaps.

Stone axes of two kinds have been found — the celt or grooveless axe which was probably set in a hole in its club-like handle, and the grooved axe, around whose groove was wrapped a handle of withes. Pestles are cylindrical stone implements used for crushing corn and herbs, probably in wooden mortars, though stone mortars, mere slabs with cup-shaped depressions, alone survive in the shell heaps to-day, the wooden ones having long since been destroyed. I do not think the long stone pestles were used in the stone mortars, their place being taken by flat cobbles. These implements, called muller, often show long use and wear, and have been found resting on the mortars. Hammerstones are often found, usually mere natural cobbles battered by use, but sometimes slightly pitted on one or both sides to keep the fingers from slipping. Another style of implement having a shallow pit and slight encircling groove may have been hafted and used as a maul. Stones showing traces of being pounded upon are called anvils, and flat pebbles notched on opposite edges for the cord, were used as net-sinkers. Sometimes net-sinkers were grooved. Large cobbles chipped to an edge probably served as hand-axes or choppers and split stones and large flakes were slightly altered for use as hoes and skin scrapers.

Flat tablets of stone called gorgets, with one or more perforations, were probably used as ornaments. Crescent-shaped flat stones, notched in the middle and usually of red limonite, occur, and are classed with the drilled "banner stones" or "ceremonials" of unknown use. I have never discovered any of the drilled variety in a shell heap, but have heard of their being found. Occasional fragments of cooking vessels made of soapstone are obtained from the shell heaps — vessels that were long and shallow, with a projecting knob on each and beneath which supporting stones could be placed when the pot was on the fire.

I know of but few stone pipes that have been found in perfect condition in or near the shell heaps of this region. One was discovered near Inwood, on Manhattan Island and is now in the possession of Mr. Bolton (Plate XVII); the other came from a child's grave near a shell heap at Tottenville, Staten Island, and was collected by Mr. G. H. Pepper (Plate IX). It is a beautiful specimen of the "monitor" or "platform" type and appears to be made of steatite. Several other pipes of stone, one of the so-called trumpet type have also been found in this cemetery while several fragments were found on the surface. Pieces of red and black soft stones such as limonite and graphite, deeply scratched for paint are numerous in some shell heaps.

The only metallic objects found that date back before the coming of the Whites are bits of copper pounded out flat and rolled into the shape of cylindrical beads. Even these are rare. Bone and deer antler implements were extensively used by the New York seacoast Indians and are often found in the shell heaps. Awls are the most abundant of these and exhibit all degrees of elaboration and finish, from the mere sharpened splinter of bone up to the finely rounded and polished implement showing little of the bone's original surface. They were undoubtedly used in sewing as the shoemaker uses his awl to-day. Often the joint of a bone has been left to serve as a handle for the awl. Bird bones were sometimes used, but deer bone was the favorite material. Occasionally awls show grooving or perforation for suspension, in which case they were probably hung on a string about their owner's neck (Fig. 7).

Broad, flat, bone needles sometimes made of the curved surface of a rib occur in small numbers, but are usually broken across the eye. The Sauk and Fox and other western tribes use such needles for making mats of cat-tail flags.

At the Shinnecock Hills, barbs suitable for tying on fish spears were made of bone, as were sometimes arrow points, the latter fashioned so as to use a part of the marrow canal as a socket for the shaft. A bone implement resembling a draw shave, probably used for removing the hair from skins, was made by cutting away a portion of a deer's leg bone so as to leave a narrow blade in the middle with the joints at both ends to serve as handles. Bird bones were made into beads or tubes and beaver teeth into knives.

The antlers of deer were found useful as material for the implements of the Indian's daily life. Arrow points were made by sharpening an antler prong, cutting it off and drilling out the base of the cone thus formed to receive the shaft. Sometimes a projection was left on the side to serve as a barb. Near the shell heaps at Tottenville, Staten Island, Mr. G. H. Pepper found three human skeletons, among whose bones were twenty-three arrow points, all but three of them, of bone and antler. One barbed antler point had actually penetrated a rib, the point projecting on the inside (Plate III). Antler points in process of manufacture and antlers from which prongs have been cut are frequent in the shell heaps.

The exact use of the cylinders of antler so often found, is not definitely known, but it is thought they may have been used as flaking tools, held between the stone blade and the hammerstone to be worked. Some antler prongs show signs of having been used to remove fine scales of quartz or flint by pressure against the edge of the implement to be finished. A few wedges of antler have been obtained — long, and often showing the natural curve of the horn. The edge has been made from one side only, after the fashion of a chisel. A curious and, as far as I know, unique implement in this region, was found at Dosoris, near Glen Cove, Long Island. A prong had been cut from an antler and squared at the thick end which was divided from the rest by a notch having a flat-topped projection. On this, five parallel lengthwise grooves had been cut. The implement must have been a stamp or marker used to draw parallel lines — perhaps on pottery and showed excellent workmanship.

Cups or bowls were made of turtle shell, with the rim cut straight and the inside scraped smooth. Fragments of these are common, but perfect specimens are seldom seen. At Pelham Bay Park, one of these objects was found, having a double row of small perforations crossing it diagonally — for what purpose it is impossible to say — it may perhaps have been used as a rattle.

Shell, although the chief component of the deposits marking the old village sites does not seem to have figured much as a material for the making of implements. A few shells have been found that show signs of use as scrapers, others have had large, round holes made in them for some unknown reason. Among the shells so perforated are those of the oyster, soft clam, and periwinkle (*Busycon carica*). Shell beads are sometimes discovered merely Olivella or Marginella shells as a rule, with holes rubbed in, to facilitate stringing. Nothing is rarer than a finished wampum bead, although on the Iroquoian sites of western New York these are found by the tens of thousands, unfinished beads occur, however, though not abundantly.

Next to the shells themselves and the split animal bones, in point of quantity, are the pieces of broken pottery — the countless fragments that are scattered throughout most shell heaps — the remains of the cooking and water vessels of the ancient people. Very few pots have survived in perfect condition, but now and then all or most of the pieces of a vessel are discovered in a pit where it has been crushed by the weight of the earth. Then the fragments may be fitted and glued together and a complete jar is the result.

For convenience sake, I divide the ancient vessels found about New York City into two classes — Algonkin and Iroquois. The Algonkin pot is more or less pointed on the bottom, and there is no raised rim or constricted neck. The decoration on this style of ware is often composed of impressions of twigs wrapped with cord, but parallel lines and chevrons drawn with a sharp point are not uncommon. Any attempt at the human face on these vessels is rare, but a few have been found. The ware is usually coarse. The Iroquois pot, on the other hand, has a round bottom, with a much constricted neck and a raised rim, often rising in a series of points. The decoration is usually confined to this raised rim, and the angle or points frequently show elaboration of the design or the rude conventional representation of the human face. Patterns composed of combinations of parallel lines and notches prevail, and thin, well made pottery is the rule. I call this style "Iroquois" because such pottery is abundant on eastern Iroquois sites, and exists in Westchester County, where intercourse with that people was probable; while it is not so common on the neighboring western end of Long Island and becomes more and more rare toward the eastern end, where Iroquoian influence was less strong, as is the case on Staten Island, where it occurs most frequently on the northern end which was most open to Iroquois inroads, in the early days. Among the thousands of potsherds found by the Museum expedition to Shinnecock Hills which is on the eastern end of Long Island, there was not one piece of the Iroquois type. Near Trenton, New Jersey, the Iroquois pottery is almost unknown and the Algonkin type prevails. I do not claim the pottery of the Iroquois style found near New York City was made by that people but that it shows their influence.

Both varieties are usually tempered with sand or pounded shells or mica mixed with the clay. In several instances pots have been found with cracks on both sides of which holes had been bored for the purpose of lacing the fissure together and preventing further spread. Many sherds and vessels bear imprints of rude fabric and cord as if the jar had been modelled in a hole with the cloth as protection against the earth or as if the pot had been patted with a paddle covered with cloth or cord.[1] Bowls and very small pots are rare. One of the latter was found at Pelham Bay Park, split in half, lengthwise. It had been used since the break occurred, for the broken edges were worn smooth.

Pipes were also made of baked clay with short thick stems usually set at an obtuse angle to the bowl — sometimes on the same plane with it. The bowl is often highly decorated in the same fashion as the pottery. Such pipes are more common on Long Island and Staten Island than in Westchester County. Stone pipes of both trumpet and platform, or monitor types, occur.

Among the animal bones found are those of the elk, deer, black bear, lynx, wolf (?), dog, beaver, raccoon, woodchuck, skunk, mink and squirrel. Wild turkey and other birds, several kinds of turtle, the snake, the crab, the shark, sturgeon and other fish were also represented. These were undoubtedly the creatures whose meat and skins were used by the Indians. Shells of almost every species common to these waters have been found, and show another source of food supply. Vegetable substances from the shell heaps include nuts, acorns, calamus roots, and corn, all preserved by charring. Charred wood is frequent.

In the upper or more recent layers of some shell heaps, are occasionally found relics showing contact with the Whites. These consist mainly of gun-flints and broken white clay pipes of the sort traded to the Indians by the early settlers.

The nearest shell heap, readily accessible to New Yorkers, is situated on the northern extremity of Manhattan Island opposite Spuyten Duyvil Station at a place called Cold Spring. This has been badly disturbed by collectors and shows its original form in a few places only. It is thought that the canoes which attacked Hendrick Hudson's ship, the Half-Moon, came from this village. Many of the specimens in the Chenoweth Collection at the Museum were found here.

Ancient encampments were plenty in what is now Pelham Bay Park, and shell heaps attesting the fact are scattered all along the shores. One of these, near "Jack's Rock" was explored for the Museum in 1899. The shell heap itself yielded little, but the pits near by and on the adjoining knolls contained much of interest, including three skeletons and a quantity

---

[1] See Holmes, Aboriginal Pottery of Eastern United States, 20th Annual Report of the Bureau of American Ethnology, p. 73.

of pottery, together with many bone and stone implements. These knolls are mentioned by R. P. Bolton in his "History of Westchester County" as a burial place of the Siwanoy Indians — one of the few cases in which "Indian Cemetries" have proven anything but the burial grounds of the early White settlers. The collection found here is now at the Museum.

The street car line from Bartow to City Island passes two large glacial boulders on a knoll just south of the road. Beyond this knoll, running down to the salt meadow, lies another shell heap only partly explored. Here, were found stone and bone implements, part of a pot, and the usual material.

One of the deepest and oldest shell heaps near New York lies within the Greater City, at Weir Creek Point, Throgg's Neck, not far from Westchester. In the lower layers, sometimes thirty-eight inches below the surface, were found a number of archaic-looking arrow points mainly of the "lozenge-shape" type, and some very rude pottery. One jar, as shown by the fragments recovered, must have had a flat bottom — an unusual feature in this vicinity where the ancient vessels generally have rounded or pointed bottoms. Mr. Ernest Volk discovered at Trenton, New Jersey, a portion of a similar pot under circumstances pointing to great antiquity, so it seems probable that this form is an old one. Implements of bone and antler, a native copper bead, and rude hammerstones, anvils and net-sinkers, were found, many of them heavily encrusted with shell-lime. Hearths and ash-beds were frequent, but pits were rare. In fact, no typical pits were found here, the nearest being on the grounds of the Century Golf Club, some distance away, where there were several. One of these had a cyst of stones near its bottom, containing the bones of two young dogs, with many deer bones and sturgeon scales imbedded in coal-black earth.

Almost directly across the Sound from Pelham Bay Park is Port Washington, Long Island. There, a large Indian village once stood, situated near the mouth of a salt creek, one mile north of the town on what is now the property of the Goodwin Sand Company. As might be expected, there is a spring near by, and the village site fronts south, a very good situation for a settlement. The principal shell heap is roughly, 200 feet in diameter, though only about one foot deep. It is overlaid, however, by another foot of soil disturbed by plowing.

Near this deposit on the land side were 101 pits, some of them beneath the shell heap itself. Many of these contained interesting relics and seventeen of them human skeletons. Sometimes three infants, an infant and an adult, or two adults were found in the same grave. The bodies were never laid out straight, as is the custom to-day but were usually buried on the side, with knees drawn up and hands near the face. No trace of any boxes or wrappings were found, but it is probable that the corpses were bundled in mats or skins. The skeletons usually lay within three feet of the surface and seldom were any relics found with them. One child's skeleton had three beads of "Olivella" shells near its neck; another had been buried just above a large dog, whose strained position suggested burial alive. An adult skeleton lay on a bed of shells, below which were found the bones of a young dog with an arrow point among the ribs, as if the animal had been shot to accompany its master on "the long journey." A fire had evidently been kindled on this grave, for there was a small ash-bed near the surface. Similar ash-beds were found on other graves. The upper skeleton of one double burial lay in good order with the bones in their natural position, while the lower was completely disarticulated and the bones mixed, one of the ribs was even within the skull. No feasible explanation of this has been offered and probably never will be. One cannot help wishing that those bones could speak and tell their story. War and violence existed then as now, for one skeleton was found with skull crushed as if by a blow, while another was headless. A smashed skull found in a pit ten feet away probably belonged to the latter. Many pits had ash-beds, some dog skeletons and some charred nuts and calamus roots.

A large number of stone and bone implements of many kinds were obtained, together with a nearly perfect pottery vessel found inverted in a pit, several incomplete pots and a vast number of fragments. Broken stems of terra cotta pipes were not uncommon, but bowls were rare. In one case, a bowl and stem were found which could be fitted together. Among the bowl fragments was one which represented a human head, probably broken from the front of the pipe.

There were pits and shells scattered about the vicinity and on the top of a neighboring knoll, where they had been exposed by digging for sand. Some loose adult bones rolling down the bank and the protruding skeletons of two children attracted my attention to the place.

There are many shell heaps about Oyster Bay, especially in Center Island and along Millneck Creek toward Bayville and Locust Valley. At Matinecock, near the latter town, is the one that was explored for the Museum. This fronted eastward on a little swampy brook flowing into the Peter's Creek branch of Millneck Creek. The deposit was rather large but seldom more than eighteen inches deep; and pits were not numerous, neither did they generally contain much of interest. The only human bone found was a small piece of skull. Many of the usual stone and bone implements and ornaments were secured however, including a grooved axe and a perforated gorget. Pottery was abundant, but no whole vessels were found.

Beneath some grand old trees that must have been standing in Indian days was found another shell heap, on Mr. James G. Price's place at Dosoris Pond, near Glen Cove. This attained the depth of 41 inches, showing that the Indian wigwam had stood in the little hollow beside the brook, many years, probably generations. For many years the Prices had in their possession the Indian deed to their property, signed by the marks of its former aboriginal owners. On the hill behind the main shell heap is located a smaller one, and here many human bones were found — parts of several skeletons. The most important relics discovered in the main shell heap, were the unusual antler implement with parallel grooves probably used by the Indian potter to draw decorations on her vessels, and a series of cores of columellae of the periwinkle shell (*Busycon carica* and *canaliculatum*) showing the different steps in the manufactures of white wampum, from the almost unworked shells to the ground and smoothed cylinders partly cut in lengths suitable for beads. A number of these were found bunched together with a white quartz flake and a small bone awl, as if they had been in a bag. Quantities of the usual relics were found.

Shell heaps, while abundant along the seacoast are seldom found inland except on salt creeks or other streams having access to salt water. They may be seen all along the east shore of the Hudson River at more or less frequent intervals up as far as Peekskill, and on Croton Point and between Nyack and Hook Mountain on the west shore they attain considerable size. There are a few small deposits, however, composed mainly of brook clams (Unio) situated on fresh water lakes in the interior of Westchester County. One of these, near White Plains, on the north shore of Little Rye Pond was examined for the Museum. The shells were much decayed and averaged about one foot deep. Two pits of the common sort were formed, one containing a raccoon skeleton and the other beaver bones and pottery fragments. In the shell layer were animal bones, broken pottery and bone implements, scattered stone implements and a few marine shells. It looks as if two or three lodges had stood here for a long time in the days when beaver and deer were plenty. Several somewhat similar camping places have been found

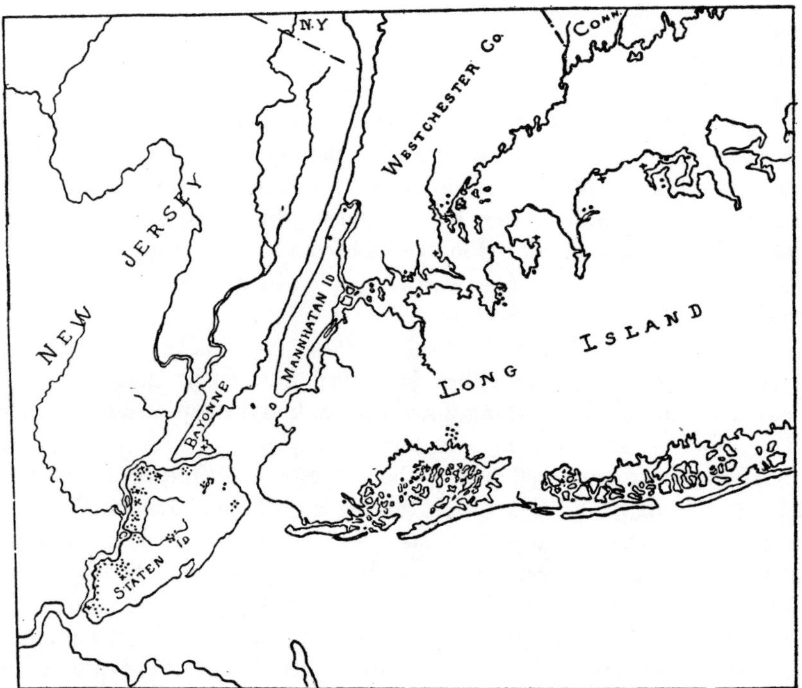

Fig. 29. Map, Giving the Locations of Shell Deposits. Those marked + have been explored by the writer.

about this lake and the adjoining Big Rye Pond, but shells were not so plentiful in these — not enough to call them shell heaps.

There are many shell heaps on Staten Island and these are described at length in another part of this volume. Shell heaps occur or did occur on Constable Hook, New Jersey, and at intervals between there and Jersey City along the western shore of New York Bay.

The foregoing discussion is based mainly upon the Museum explorations of the writer in Long Island and Westchester County. The shell deposits actually excavated are indicated on the map, together with the locations of all other deposits so far noted by us (Fig. 29). This map is no doubt far from complete.

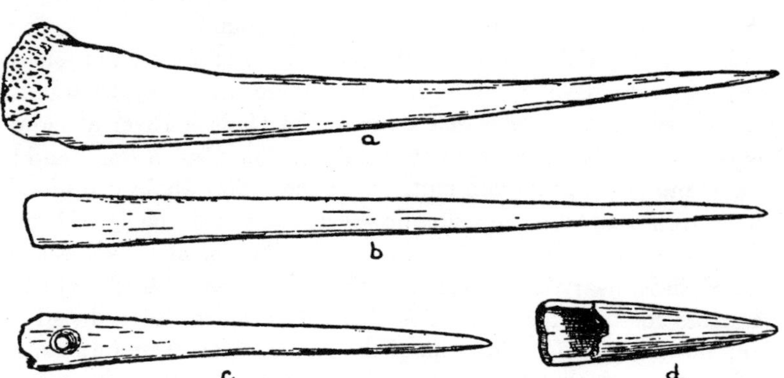

Fig. 7 *a* (1–3942), *b* (1–3944), *c*, *d* (Bolton and Calver Collection). Implements of Bone and Horn, Van Cortlandt Park. Length of *a*, 14.5 cm.

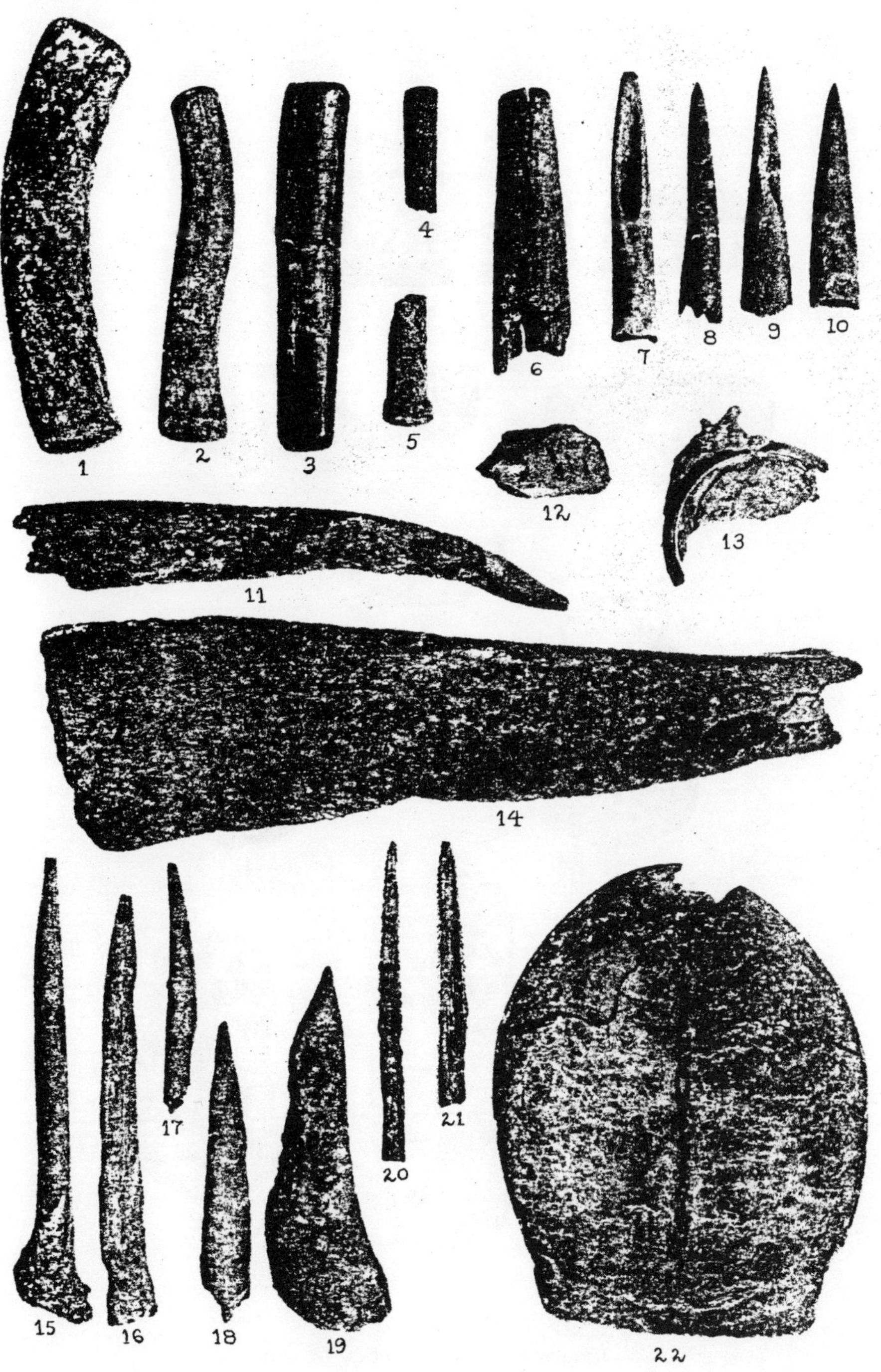

Bone and Antler Tools.

Relics from Manhattan Island.

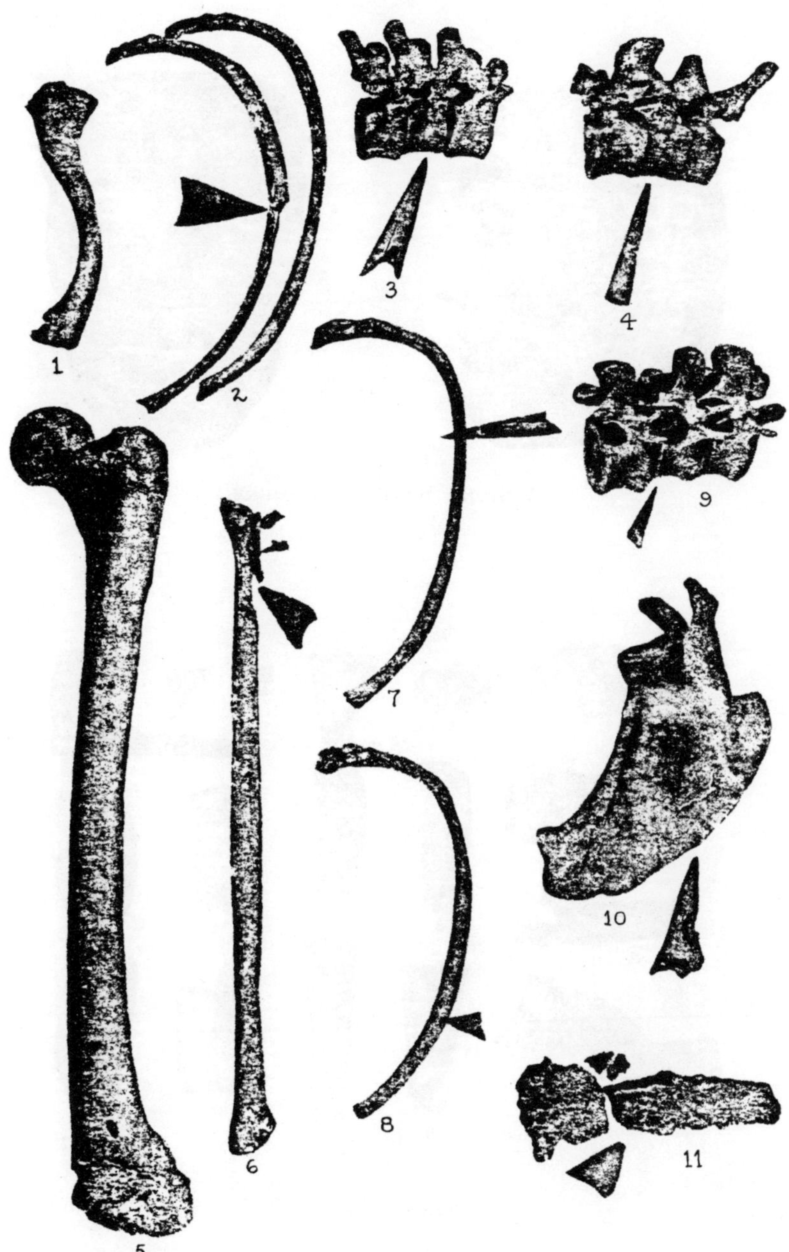

Position of Points among Bones — Tottenville.

A Stone Head — Grasmere.

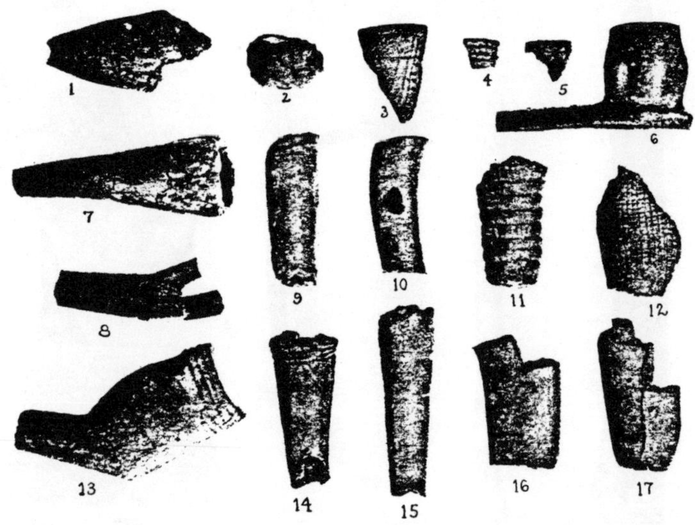

Tobacco Pipes.

Knives and Scrapers.

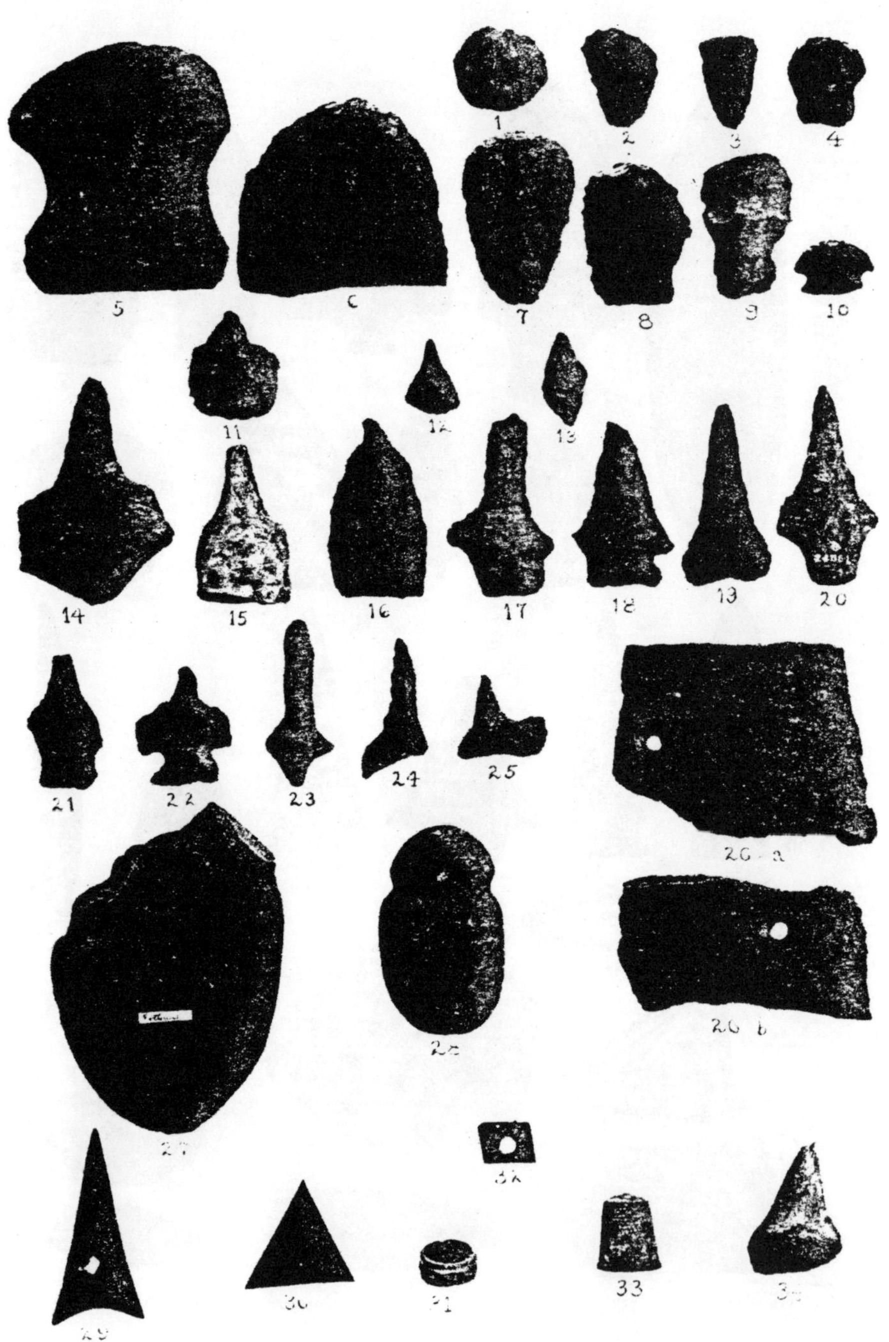

Drills, Scrapers and other Objects.

Banner Stones.

A MONTAUK CEMETERY AT EASTHAMPTON, LONG ISLAND

BY

FOSTER H. SAVILLE

FOREWORD

URING the summer of 1917, Dr Henry O'Brien, of Brooklyn, drew the attention of Mr Foster H. Saville, of the Museum of the American Indian, Heye Foundation, to the fact that evidences of an Indian cemetery had been found near the town of Easthampton, on the southern shore near the eastern end of Long Island, New York. On investigation Mr Saville found that on the farm of Mr Frank N. Nelson, in excavating for the foundation of a chicken-house there had been uncovered in January, 1914, several human skeletons, with accompaniments.

Through the generosity of Mr James B. Ford, a trustee of the Museum, excavation of the site, which was found to be along the slope of a sandy knoll, was made possible. Permission to conduct the investigation having been courteously granted by Mr Nelson, work was commenced on October 22, 1917, and was terminated, owing to inclement weather, on December 17, after twenty-four skeletons and six fireplaces had been exposed. In 1918 the work was continued for ten days in May and five days in November, when it was finished. Fifty-eight burials in all were found: thirty-nine by the Museum expedition, seventeen by Mr Nelson when the original excavation for the foundation referred to was made, and two by Dr O'Brien at the same time. The accompaniments recovered include a large assortment of early Colonial material that had been traded with the Indians, one of the most interesting of which is a glass bottle on which has been scratched the name of Wabetom, a Montauk chief.

Acknowledgments are due to Messrs Frank N. Nelson and Frank R. Worthington for the gift to the Museum of the objects found in association with the first skeletons unearthed, and also to Messrs J. Thomas Gardiner, Joseph Osborn, and Samuel Gregory, all of Easthampton, and to Mr Nat Booth of Southold, Long Island, for their assistance and interest in the investigation. The Museum is indebted also to Mr Reginald Pelham Bolton for the identification of some of the Colonial objects found associated with the graves, as well as for the survey on which the accompanying map (pl. II) is based. The pen-drawings reproduced in the paper were prepared by Mr William Baake.

GEORGE G. HEYE,
Director.

Reprinted from Museum of the American Indian: Heye Foundation, INDIAN NOTES AND MONOGRAPHS, Vol. 2, No. 3, 1920.

A MONTAUK CEMETERY AT EASTHAMPTON, LONG ISLAND

By Foster H. Saville

HISTORY

EASTHAMPTON, the most easterly town on Long Island, New York, was first settled in 1648. The town includes the peninsula of Montauk and Gardiners island, as well as the hamlets of Amagansett, Devon, Naprague, Montauk, Freetown, Springs, Wainscot, Accabonack, Jericho, Georgica, and Appaquogue, in addition to other places still retaining a form of their Indian names, such as Copecs, Munchog, Wamponamon, and Pantigo.

The Indian cemetery herein described is situated about two miles east of the village of Easthampton, on the Amagansett road, on the upper part of what is locally known as Pantigo Hill (pl. I). The meaning of the name *Pantigo* is obscure.[1] Regarding it, the late William Wallace Tooker wrote:

> "The early settlers frequently gave names to localities from some local happening. Among such names we find 'Hard Scrabble,' 'Toilsome,' 'Scuttle Hole,' 'Whippoorwill,' etc. Pantigo, supposed to be aboriginal, evidently belongs to the same class, and is probably the English 'pant-I-go.' In this derivation Hon. Henry B. Hedges, the East Hampton historian, concurs."

SAVILLE — EASTHAMPTON PL. I

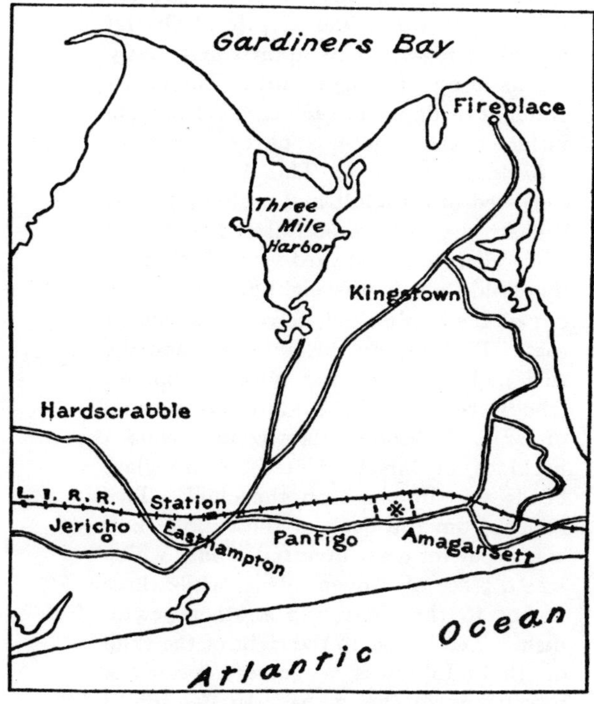

EASTHAMPTON AND VICINITY

Mr J. N. B. Hewitt, of the Bureau of American Ethnology, however, kindly investigated the meaning of this name, with the following result:

> "It may be assumed that the name [Pantigo] is of Algonquian Indian origin, and allowance must be made for a marked measure of Anglicization, and a lack of knowledge of the historical reasons for its use must be admitted; nevertheless, we may conjecture that the name originally meant, the "tidal river or inlet which is crosswise or athwart the view."

If one stands at the summit of Pantigo hill, a view may be had of the Atlantic, and of Three Mile Harbor and Gardiners Bay, and this fact seems to bear out the meaning of the name as suggested by Mr Hewitt, Three Mile Harbor being the tidal inlet referred to.

The first historical record of Pantigo is found in a deed from William Edwards to his daughter, dated December 18, 1669,[2] in which is conveyed "all the Meadow ground at ackobonck and ackobonck neck and that Lott at pantego Robert Daiton Lying East and Mr Chatfield Lying west."

The Montauk Indians in early days had a burial ground on what is now Main street in the town of Easthampton, only a short distance south of the site of the church cemetery.[3] During the smallpox epidemic which commenced in 1660 and continued for some years, various laws were enacted by the white settlers to prevent the spread of the disease among themselves. From these laws[4] the following is extracted:

> "It is ordered that noe Indian shall come to towne in to the street after sufficient notice upon penalty of paying 5s. or be whipped untill they be free of the small poxe; but they may come when they have corn on the back side and call: and if any English or Indian servant shall go to their wigwams they shall suffer the same punishment."

From this order it is evident that, being unable to use their old cemetery, the Montauk were compelled to establish a new one, hence it is probable that burials were first made on Pantigo hill at that time. None of the records of Easthampton, however, allude to such use of the site.

A glass bottle of English manufacture, found in one of the graves, bears the name "Wobetom" scratched on its shoulder (pl. v). In the Easthampton Town Records, vol. II, p. 213 (Book G, p. 84), is an indenture dated July 25, 1657, conveying from the sachems of the Montauk Indians to the trustees of the town of Easthampton a large part of their land.

Among the various signatures to this deed is "Wobetom, his mark X." It is thus evident that Wobetom was a Montauk chief. Thirteen years after the purchase of Montauk, namely in 1670, a paper was negotiated by John Mulford, Ritcherd Straten, and Tho. Backer (Records of Easthampton, I, p. 330) "wheare obadia the engiane was hiered to keepe the cattell att mantake A munth his munth being out we have hiered wabatiene the engien to keape a nother munth: for the same wages obadia kepte that is ten shillings by weak: he keerfully to kepe them beyond the forte pond he begining the 24 Day of this instant June 1670."

Again, in the same record (p. 381) is an agreement dated December 2, 1675, between some of the settlers and Indians to enter upon a whaling venture. In the document, among Indians enumerated, occurs the name "Awaupetun," and among the signatures thereto is "Wahpetum" X his mark & seale." As no similar name occurs in both parts of the document, it may be assumed that the two names pertain to the same individual, or Wobetom, especially as there is little consistency in the spelling of Indian names at this period, not only on Long Island but throughout the colonies. The following extract is from the same records.[5]

"This Indenture made this 12 day of August in the yeare of our Lord 1683 betwene Richard Stretton of Easthampton on ye one partie And John Indian sonn of Wobbeton on the other partie as witnesseth."

This is the last mention of Wobetom, hence it is probable that his death occurred not long afterward.

Two English coins bearing the date 1728 were found with one of the burials at Pantigo, which suggest the ultimate period at which the cemetery was used, although, of course, a number of years may have elapsed between the date of the coins and the time they were deposited in the grave. If the burial accompanied with the bottle bearing the name of Wobetom was that of this chief, the cemetery was in use, in all probability, from the latter part of the seventeenth century to the early part, if not the middle, of the eighteenth century.

THE SKELETONS

Before systematic excavation was commenced by the Museum in October, 1917, Mr Nelson had uncovered seventeen skeletons while improving his land in January, 1916, and Dr O'Brien had taken out two others. These, with the thirty-nine found during the investigations by the Museum, give a total of fifty-eight. The burials were all found within an area approximately 105 feet north and south by 70 feet east and west (pl. II).

Of the thirty-nine burials of which accurate data were kept, thirty-seven were of adults and two of children; twenty-one were flexed and seventeen were interred in an extended position, while in one case it was impossible to determine the position, owing to the disintegrated condition of the bones. Thirty of the burials were directed eastwardly, six northeastwardly, and three southwestwardly. Twenty-one of the skeletons presented indications of having been wrapped in trade blankets or in other textiles, or in skin or bark, while in eighteen of the graves other accompaniments were found. A number of the skeletons were in poor condition, in many instances only traces of the bones being encountered, while others pulverized on exposure. Fortunately, however, it was possible to recover many of the bones of a number of the skeletons, including several of the skulls.

A description of the skeletons that were accompanied with artifacts follows. Unless otherwise noted, the skeletons are those of adults whose skulls were directed eastwardly. As the sand in which the interments were made had been greatly shifted by wind, the depth of burial should be regarded as approximate only and as in no wise significant. The measurement of depth in each case is from the surface to the uppermost part of the skull.

Skeletons 7 and 8.—This double burial consisted of an adult and a child, 4½ ft. beneath the surface, both flexed, with the adult directed eastwardly, and that of the child, which was eight inches to the left of the adult skull, toward the southeast. Both lay on the right side and the two had been covered with a blanket. About the neck of the adult was a string of large, dark-blue, glass beads, while a necklace of large, faceted, amber-glass beads was in place on the child. Two inches from the back of the child's skull was a pewter dish, inverted, under which was a piece of woven fabric, while three inches to the right was another pewter dish. Ten inches to the right of the skull of the adult was a pottery vessel of unusual form (fig. 1, *a*). In the top of the receptacle was the base of a Colonial earthenware vessel with the edge ground. Under and around both skeletons were a large number of white, black, blue, and green glass beads, and some red glass beads with black ends, also three large, light-blue, glass beads, three melon-shaped, corrugated, glass beads, and twelve metal buttons. Eighteen inches above the burial was a white quartz arrow blank.

Skeleton No. 9.—Four feet below the surface, flexed, lying on its right side on a blanket. Four inches east of the skull was a clay trade pipe marked "R. T." (pl. IX, *a*), as well as a fragment of an iron knife in a wooden handle (pl. XIII, *a*), and some small blue glass beads strung on a cord.

Skeleton No. 10.—Four feet below the surface, flexed on its right side on a piece of deerskin, and covered with bark and a blanket. Near the skull was a small deposit of red paint. Four inches from the right side of the skull was a clay trade pipe. Eleven inches beyond the skull was a glass bottle, as well as fragments of a pewter spoon. Six inches to the left of the skeleton was an iron kettle, containing a shallow one of the same material, in which was a small pottery vessel (fig. 1, *b*). Under the leg bones was a double-toothed brass comb with a string of blue glass and copper beads (pl. XIV, *d*), two brass buckles (pl. XIV, *a*, *c*), twenty-five pieces of wampum, fragments of a wampum belt, and five copper beads. Scattered about the skeleton were a large number of strung blue and white glass beads, also some of copper. Eighteen inches above this burial, or two and a half feet below the surface, was a white quartz arrowpoint.

Skeleton No. 13.—Four and one-half feet beneath the surface, flexed. Six inches to the right of the skull was a small green glass bottle (pl. IV, *b*), under which was a small pewter dish. Four inches farther was an iron dish, and touching this at the right was a brass one, bound with bark (pl. XI), and containing a silver-plated spoon. Under the spoon were fragments of textile, a piece of copper, and a brass thimble. Nine inches from the right leg bones was a piece of textile (the remains of a bag) on which lay a necklace of shell and copper beads, on one end of which was a brass ring containing strung white and black glass beads. Suspended from the ring is a small copper bell, attached to which is a small, round, brass box. Associated with this burial were a number of turtle-bones, a fragment of a wampum belt, and a large number of blue, white, black, and green glass beads, and some copper beads (see pl. XV).

Skeleton No. 14.—Three feet below the surface, flexed. Above and around the skeleton were a number of blue, white, and black glass beads, also buttons of lead, black glass, and brass, and copper beads.

Skeleton No. 15.—Three and one-half feet below the surface, lying on its back, legs extended. On the breast was a long, cylindrical, shell bead (fig. 3, *a*). Twelve inches to the left of the skull were fragments of a pewter dish containing a silver-plated iron spoon (pl. XII, *b*), and a brass thimble and ring (pl. XIV, *b*). With this burial were beads of copper, as well as of black, blue, and white glass, mingled with lead and glass buttons.

Skeleton No. 19.—Three feet below the surface, on its back, extended, with the top of the skull directed toward the northeast. At the occiput was a trade pipe of clay (pl. IX, *b*); around the neck were a number of black glass beads and fragments of brass pins.

Skeleton No. 21.—Four and one-half feet down, body extended on its right side, with right arm in front of face. Almost surrounding the skeleton, six inches distant, was an outline of small beach pebbles, the larger ones at the feet (pl. III). Above this burial were a great many fire-broken stones and much charcoal. Around and near the neck were numerous small glass beads; on the breast was a pin made from two English pennies, dated 1728, also a number of white and orange glass beads, and some metal buttons.

Skeleton No. 25.—Three and one-half feet below the surface, flexed, lying on a blanket. Around the remains were a number of pewter buttons, also numerous small black, blue, white, and yellow glass beads.

Skeleton No. 26.—Three and one-half feet deep, legs extended, hands under chin. Twelve inches to the left of the skull was an almost complete yellow china pitcher, three inches to the left of which was a mug of similar ware and color (pl. VII, *b*, *c*), and between the two a pewter spoon. On the right side of the skull was a razor-blade knife in a bone handle (pl. XIII, *d*), the blade resting against the frontal: at the occiput was a long metal tube (pl. XIV, *e*); under the chin a few black glass beads.

Skeleton No. 27.—A child, 2 ft. 9 in. beneath the surface, lying on its back,

SAVILLE — EASTHAMPTON PL. III

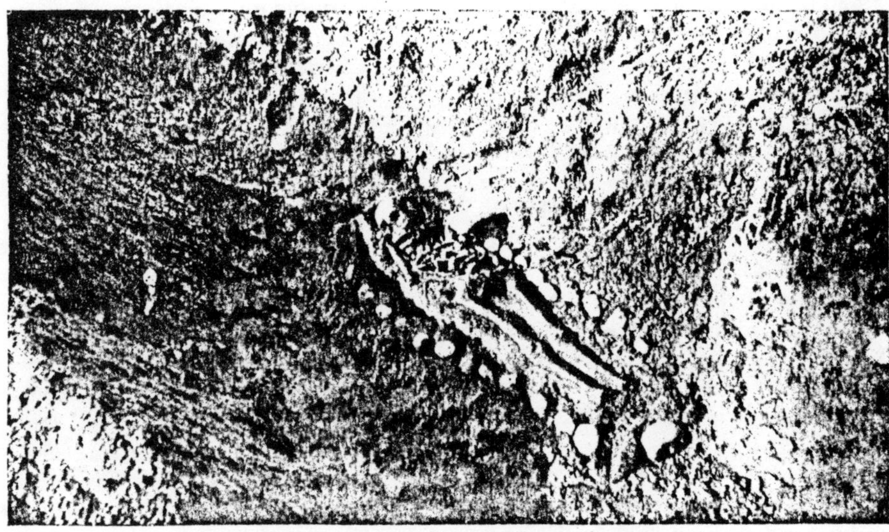

BURIAL 21, SURROUNDED WITH PEBBLES

SAVILLE — EASTHAMPTON PL. IV

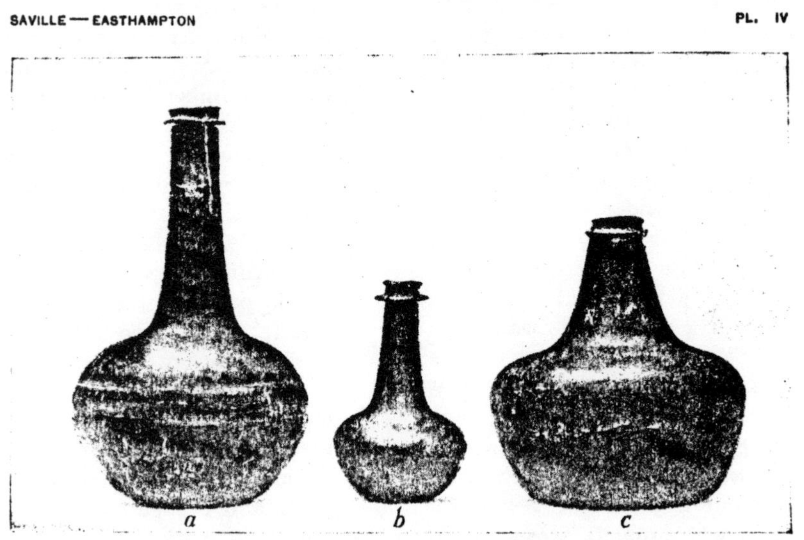

BOTTLES OF DARK-GREEN GLASS
(Height of *a*, 8⅝ in.; *b*, 4⅞ in.; *c*, 6¼ in.)

with legs extended. Near the chin were a number of black cut-glass button tops, a number of small white and dark blue glass beads, and some square white and pink barrel-shaped beads. Six inches above the burial were evidences of a fire, as the earth was discolored with small pieces of charcoal for an area of four by five feet. Skeleton No. 29 was directly beneath this burial.

Skeleton No. 28.—Three and one-half feet down, on its back, with legs extended. On the skull was a cylindrical shell bead, four inches long, and a fragment of a metal kettle containing a short-handled spoon and a long-handled one of Sheffield plate marked "R. S." (See fig. 5). Under the bowl of the shorter spoon was a small, roundish, wooden box (pl. x, *b;* fig. 6), also a few small white and blue glass beads. Near the skull were a number of small, cylindrical beads of blue glass with white stripes. A number of pewter buttons were found near the skull.

Skeleton No. 29.—Four and one-half feet in depth, flexed, lying upon a piece of skin. Around the skeleton were a number of pewter buttons. (See Skeleton No. 27.)

Skeleton No. 30.—The conditions of this burial are identical with those of Skeleton No. 29, except as to location.

Skeleton No. 31.—Two and one-half feet below the surface, legs flexed, hands at

GLASS BOTTLE WITH "WOBETOM" SCRATCHED THEREON
(Height 6¼ in.)

chin. Near the skull were a few large, black glass beads, together with a few brass pins.

Skeleton No. 32.—Two and one-half feet down, facing east, legs extended, hands across the chest. Six inches to the right of the skull were two metal dishes. Under the skeleton was the shaft-end of a stone arrowpoint. In front of the skull were traces of an iron implement, also an iron knife with a wooden handle (pl. XIII, *b*), and a spoon of Sheffield plate (pl. XII, *a*). Eighteen inches to the left of the skeleton was a small deposit of red paint.

Skeleton No. 33.—Three feet below the surface. The body lay on its right side upon a piece of fabric. The legs were extended, the hands across the chest. Six inches to the right of the skull were two iron dishes; near the left hand was an iron knife with an antler handle (pl. XIII, *c*). Eighteen inches to the left of the skeleton was a deposit of red paint covering an area of three square feet and of a maximum thickness of five inches.

Skeleton No. 35.—Two and a half feet beneath the surface, legs flexed, the hands under chin. The remains lay on the right side on a piece of fabric. In front of the skull were fragments of a pewter spoon, and six inches to the right of the skull were pieces of a small iron vessel. Ten inches above the cranium was a deposit of red paint.

Skeleton No. 39.—Three feet down, lying on its right side on a blanket, legs flexed, arms crossed, and hands covering the face. Under the knees were a number of thicknesses of fabric, probably the remains of a blanket. Near the skeleton was a deposit of red paint.

Besides the above objects found *in situ*, many were plowed up by Mr Nelson, leading to the discovery of the cemetery. The latter consisted both of articles received through trade with the English and those of aboriginal origin; among them were three clay trade pipes, four long cylindrical shell beads, a shell pendant drilled in two places for suspension, a conical shell pendant, a clamshell containing some red paint, a small rubber of hematite and another of graphite, an iron thimble perforated for suspension, three flat metal ornaments, a small woven medicine-bag, two plated

AMBER-COLORED VENETIAN GLASS PITCHER
(Height 3½ in.)

spoons, a round white crockery dish or porringer with handle (pl. VIII), a small amber-glass pitcher; the large green glass bottle with the word "Wobetom" scratched on its shoulder, a fragment of an iron knife with a wooden handle, two flint scrapers, part of a pewter spoon, an arrowpoint, and numerous buttons of metal and glass, together with almost countless glass beads. The glass bottle with the name "Wobetom," Mr Nelson relates, was from a grave which contained also a Venetian glass mug and the china dish, but close examination was not made to determine whether any additional objects accompanied this burial. Although the grave cannot be positively identified as that of the Montauk chief, it was undoubtedly that of an important and wealthy individual, as is shown by the unusual articles buried therein. On the accompanying map (pl. II), this burial is referred to as that of Wobetom, with a query.

ABORIGINAL ARTIFACTS

Stone

The only stone objects exhibiting aboriginal workmanship are two small flint scrapers and six crudely chipped arrowpoints, of which latter four are of white quartz and of the type usually found on Long Island. Other arrowpoints were found in the vicinity.

Pottery

Two pieces of aboriginal pottery were found, and, strangely enough, only one small potsherd.

Fig. 1.—Pottery vessels. (Height of *a*, 5¾ in.; of *b*, 2⅝ in.)

The larger vessel (fig. 1, *a*) is of coarse, light-brown ware, cylindrical, with a flat base. Below the rim is a row of nodes, while at one side, directly on the rim, is a knob-like handle. The only ornamentation, in addition to the nodes, is a punctate one on top and at the end of each of the nodes, and also over the handle. This embellishment seems to indicate that it was applied with the end of a reed or a small bone.

SAVILLE — EASTHAMPTON PL. VII

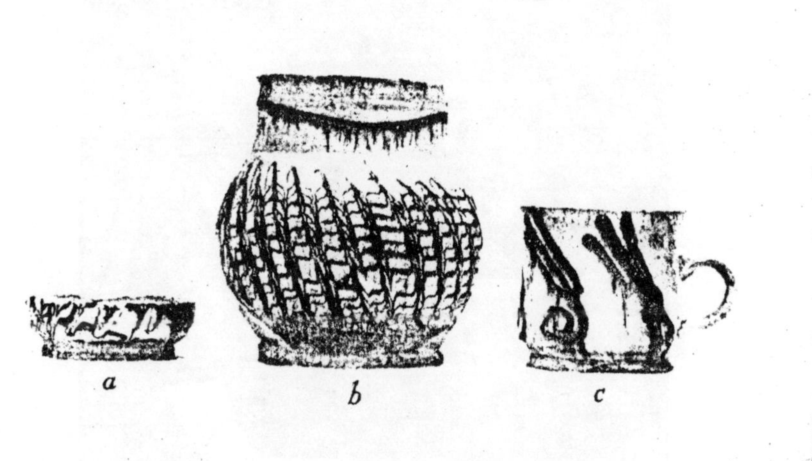

POTTERY WITH YELLOW BASE AND BLACK COMB DECORATION; PROBABLY STAFFORDSHIRE
(Diameter: *a*, 3⅝ in.; *b*, 5¾ in.; *c*, 3⅜ in.)

SAVILLE — EASTHAMPTON PL. VIII

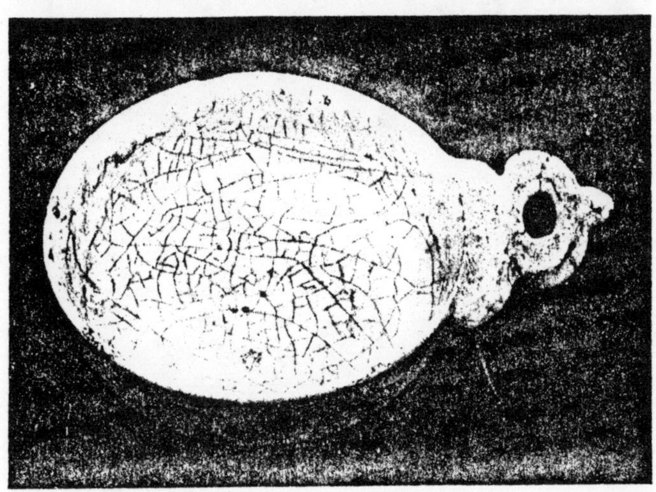

PORRINGER OF WHITE CHINA
(Diameter 7⅜ in.)

The other earthenware vessel (fig. 1, *b*) is a small, cylindrical jar, also of coarse, light-brown ware, with a flattish base and a row of nodes beneath the rim. As a part of the rim is missing, it cannot be determined whether a projection had originally been provided for use as a handle, as in the case of the larger jar. Although different in form, both specimens seem to be of the ordinary quality of earthenware found on Eastern Algonkian sites.

The potsherd referred to is small, and of plain, coarse, brown ware.

Shell

A conical shell pendant (fig. 2) was found by Mr Nelson at the time the cemetery was discovered. It is evidently made from an end of the columella of a large shell, possibly a periwinkle.

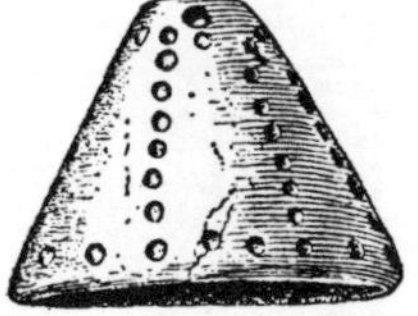

Fig. 2.—Shell Pendant (¾).

It is perforated at the top for suspension, and ornamented with a band of circular dots around both top and base; these bands are connected by seven vertical rows of eight similar marks.

Another shell pendant fashioned from an East Indian money cowry (*Cypraea moneta* Linn.) is drilled in two places at one end for suspension.

Six tubular shell beads were recovered, of which examples are illustrated in fig. 3. A clam-shell containing traces

SAVILLE — EASTHAMPTON PL. IX

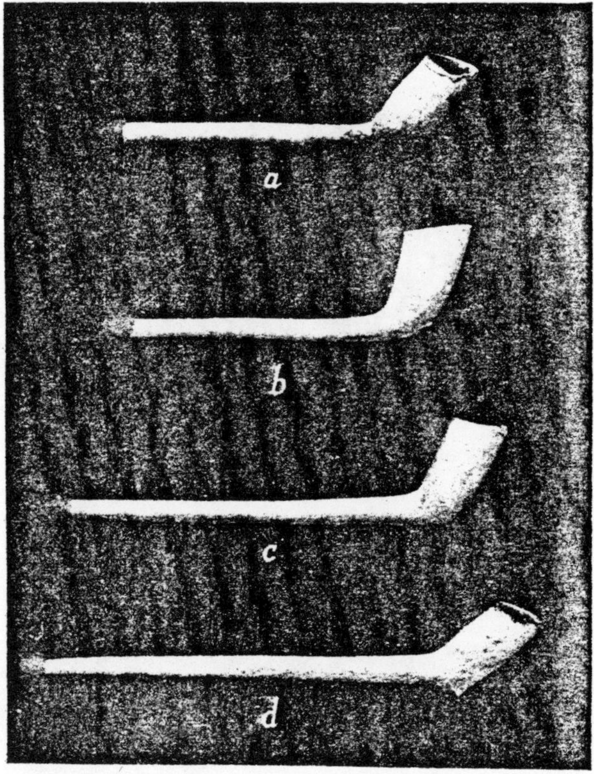

WHITE CLAY TRADE PIPES
(Length: *a*, 5⅜ in.; *d*, 7½ in.)

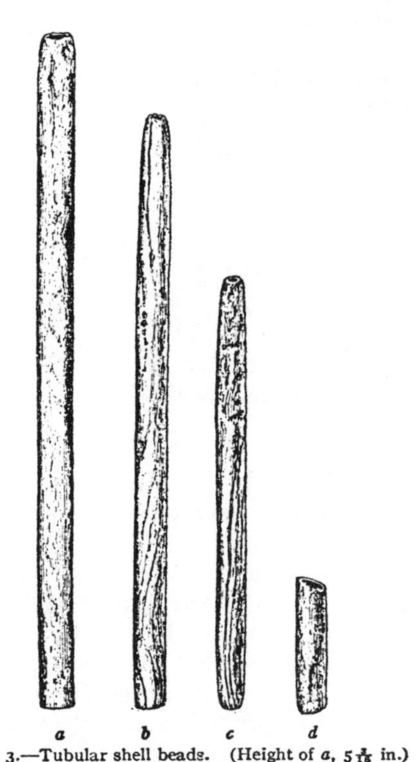

FIG. 3.—Tubular shell beads. (Height of *a*, 5 $\frac{3}{16}$ in.)

SAVILLE — EASTHAMPTON PL. X

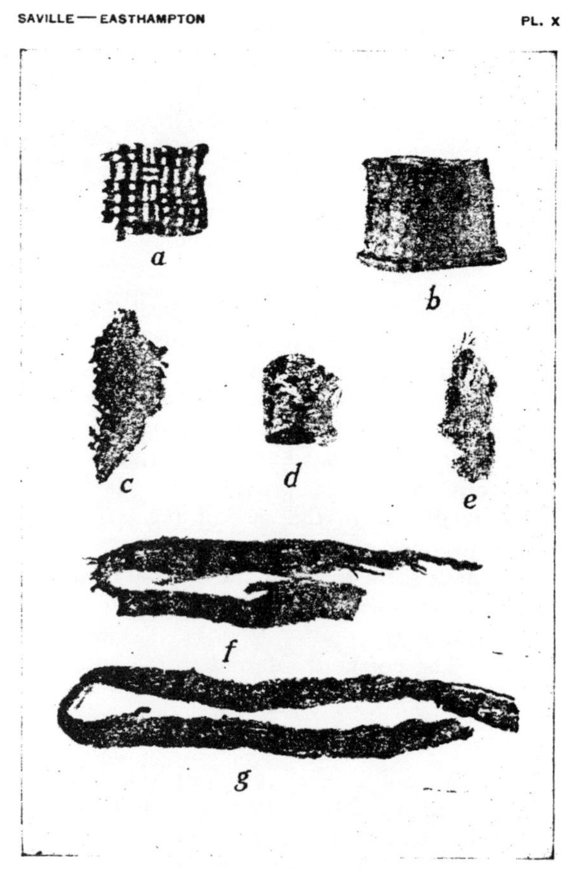

VARIOUS TRADE OBJECTS

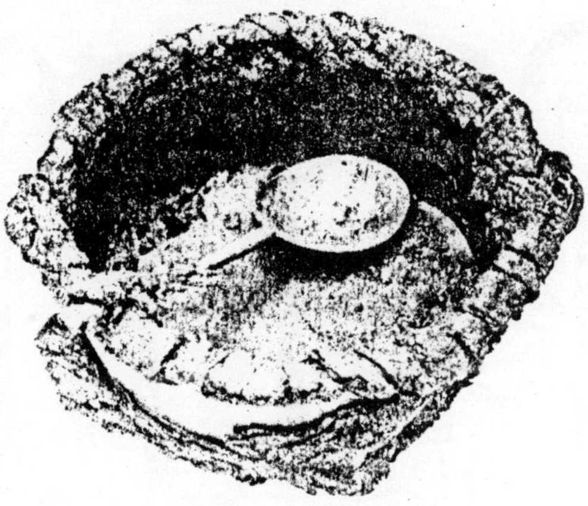

BRASS KETTLE WITH BARK WRAPPING
(Diameter 6½ in.)

of red paint was found in one of the graves.

As noted above in describing the graves, various strands and a few single wampum beads were found in association with the graves.

Pigments

There was also recovered a small, triangular, hematite rubber, and in several of the graves was found some red oxide of iron.

TRADE ARTICLES

Glass

Three glass bottles (pl. IV) had been deposited as burial accompaniments; they are all of dark greenish glass, and on the shoulder of one, as previously mentioned, is scratched the name "Wobetom" (pl. IV, *c*, and V).

The *Transactions of the Cumberland and Westmoreland Antiquarian and Archæological Society* (vol. IV, 1904, p. 213, fig. 2), and *The Collectors Manual* (p. 94, fig. 131) contain illustrations of Dutch bottles used for "schnapps," which seem to be identical in form with the bottles herein mentioned, but they are also similar to so-called "sack" bottles which were manufactured at Chiddenfold, Surrey, England, in the eighteenth century, in imitation of those imported from Holland.

Among other objects unearthed by Mr Nelson is a small amber-colored glass pitcher decorated with a band of thread-like white glass on and below the rim. Through the courtesy of Mr Arthur S. Verney, of New York City, this specimen (pl. VI) has been identified as of Venetian origin of an early date.

Some black glass buttons with metal eyes, resembling in shape the present-day shoe-buttons, although about three times as large, were found.

Twenty-five varieties of trade glass beads were found with the burials at Pantigo. They include a string of large faceted amber glass beads, and a number of large green beads covered with projections, causing them to resemble blackberries in form. Other kinds include large black globular, white oval, tiny black cylindrical with red stripes, small red cylindrical, small yellow cylindrical with green stripes, small corrugated black melon-shaped ones, small pink barrel-shaped, and small red beads with black ends. The small and large round beads are white, green, blue, black, garnet, and red. There were also found a number of circular faceted black glass objects without perforation, but which had probably been used as inlays on a variety of buttons.

Pottery

Among the objects gathered are three pieces of coarse pottery with a yellow base color and a black combed decoration (pl. VII). They consist of a fragment of a pitcher with the handle missing (*b*), a mug (*c*), and the base of a vessel the top of which has been ground off (*a*). We are informed by Mr Reginald Pelham Bolton that fragments of similar ware, which is probably Staffordshire, have been found at old Colonial sites about New York City.

SAVILLE — EASTHAMPTON PL. XII

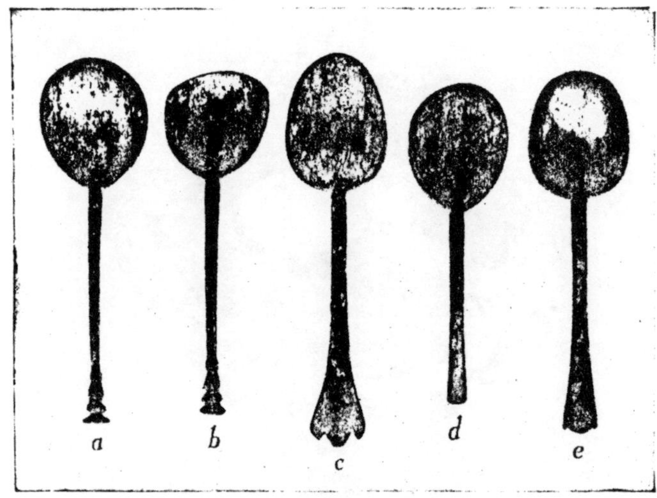

BRASS SPOONS
(The length of *a* and *e* is 6⅝ in.)

Plate VIII illustrates a white porringer of Dutch design and of early Delft manufacture.[6]

There were also found six white clay pipes (pl. IX), of the type generally traded to Indians by the early colonists. With the exception of one of the pipes (*a*), which is stamped with the letters "R. T.", they are unmarked. According to Barber[7] these were probably made by Richard Tyler, a celebrated pipe-maker in the vicinity of Bath, England, during the early part of the seventeenth century.

TEXTILES

Many fragments of textile were found, most of which consist of a blanket-like material, but there were also recovered a coarse homespun cloth, fragments of coarse and fine homespun linen, and a cloth of fine twined weave (pl. X, *c*, *e-g*). The sole of a moccasin was found, but its poor condition prohibited identification of the leather. Fragments of skin and leather were unearthed from the graves, but whether the latter were of Indian tanning is not determined.

A small medicine-bag of homespun cloth was among the objects recovered from the graves; its end was broken off, but attached to it are some strands of human hair (fig. 4).

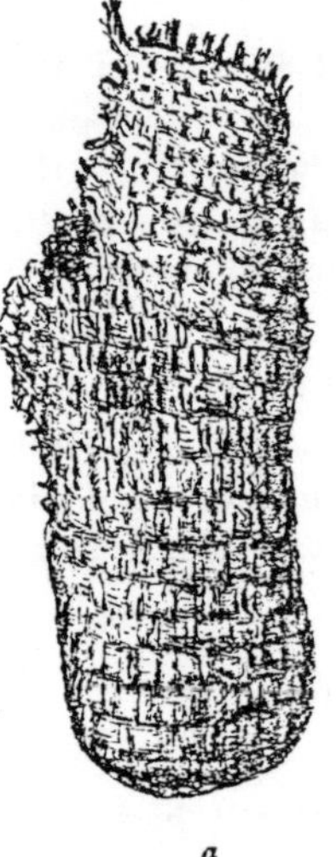

FIG. 4.—Part of a medicine-bag of cloth. (Length of *a*, 2½ in.)

METAL

Kettles.—Five metal kettles of the type often traded to the Indians in old Colonial days were recovered, four of which are of iron and the other of brass. The brass kettle (pl. XI) has been carefully covered on the rim and the base with a wrapping of bark, and when found contained a silver-plated metal spoon similar to those to be described.

Spoons.—One of the small iron kettles (fig. 5) contained two brass spoons, one of which is silver plated. Besides the spoons enumerated, five others were found (pl. XII). These are all of brass, with traces of silver plating, and are of late seventeenth and early eighteenth century manufacture.[8] They may be described as follows:

(*a*) Trefoil spoon with the hallmark in the bowl, reading "Double plate" in a circle, inside of which are the initials "R. S."; probably manufactured by Richard Sheffield about 1660.

(*b*) A slip-end Puritan spoon, the hallmark not being legible.

(*c*) Trefoil spoon, the hallmark in the bowl showing a bird with the letters "W. W."

SAVILLE — EASTHAMPTON PL. XIII

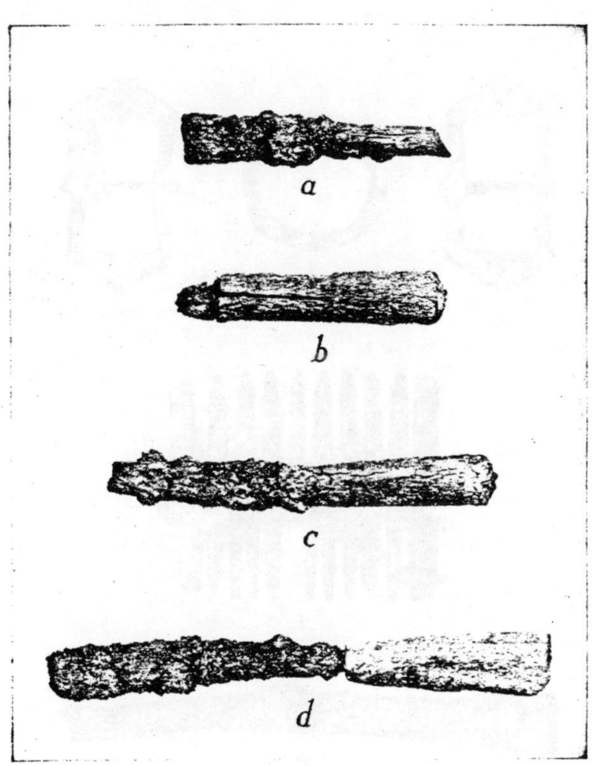

KNIVES
(The length of *a* and *b* is 4 in.)

Fig. 5.—Small iron kettle with two brass spoons.

(*d*) Seal-top, with baluster ornament, the bowl of which has been ground down. The hallmark is defaced.

(*e*) Seal-top, with baluster ornament, the hallmark in the bowl being a lion rampant with crown above and the initials "T. C."

Pewter.—There were also found two shallow pewter dishes, fragments of two pewter spoons, and some buttons of the same material.

Knives.—Parts of four knives similar in type to table knives of the present time were recovered (pl. XIII). One of these (*a*) has a fragment of its wooden handle attached; two others, (*b, c*) have their original bone handles, while the fourth (*d*) has a handle evidently made from a deer antler.

Buttons.—Several kinds of metal buttons were found, mostly of the disc type, made of pewter. There are also in the collection hemispherical buttons of brass and pewter.

Beads.—A number of copper beads, both barrel-shaped and cylindrical, were encountered; some of the latter were made from copper fragments, and in one piece of beadwork formed a cross design (pl. X, *a*) surrounded with globular black glass trade beads. Some small cylindrical brass beads were recovered.

Miscellaneous.—Among other metal objects were brass thimbles used as ornaments (pl. X, *d*), a pair of brass buckles (pl. XIV, *a*, *c*), a fragment of a small silver religious token, two English pennies of the date 1728, and the handle of a brass spoon that evidently had been cut from part of a kettle.

Miscellaneous Trade Objects

A fragment of a woven black-and-white glass bead belt was found, likewise a fragment of another woven belt consisting of the same type of

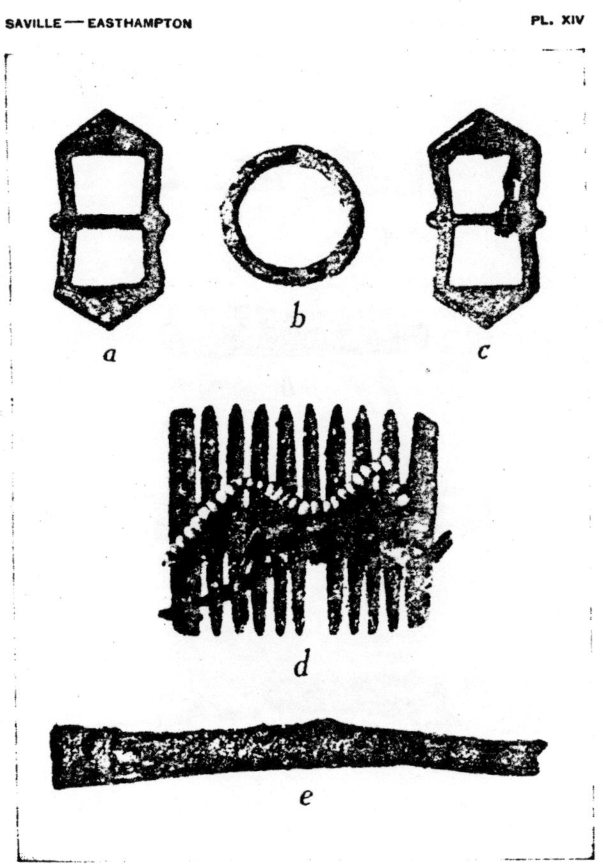

VARIOUS TRADE OBJECTS

(Diameter of *b*, 1⅛ in.)

black glass beads with small brass cylindrical ones (pl. X, *a*), as above mentioned.

A comb (pl. XIV, *d*), evidently cut from a fragment of a brass kettle, was discovered, and on top of it was a string of blue glass beads and also a couple of deerskin thongs, one of which has a barrel-shaped copper bead attached to it.

A small wooden box, with the remains of its cover in place, was found without

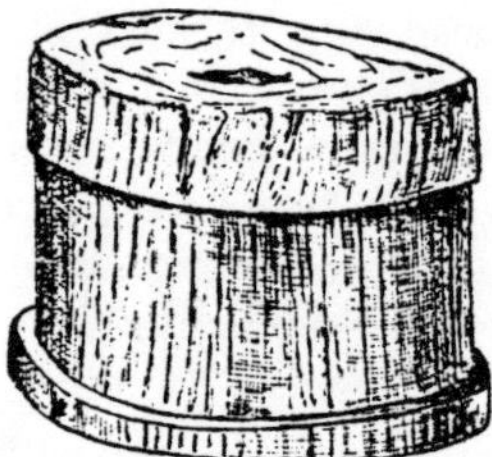

FIG. 6.—Wooden box (five-sixths actual size).

contents (pl. X, *b;* fig. 6). This receptacle had probably been circular, but was misshapen when recovered.

About nine inches from the legs of skeleton No. 13 was an ornate neck-piece in a bag, composed of barrel-shaped copper beads alternating with cylindrical beads of shell (pl. XV). At the bottom of this strand is a pendant consisting of a brass ring in which black and white glass beads have been strung, completely filling it. Pendent from the bottom of this is a copper tinkler containing an iron pellet, below which is attached a small, circular, brass box.

FIREPLACES

Six fireplaces were discovered in the northern, eastern, and southeastern parts of the burial-ground, the whole forming an angle with its apex toward the east (pl. II). As the fireplaces were much alike, a description of No. 1 will serve the purpose of all. This was eighteen inches below the surface and consisted of about forty bowlders, averaging perhaps twenty pounds in weight, much discolored by fire and arranged in the form of a circle. The fireplaces were three feet in diameter and eighteen inches in depth, and contained twelve inches of ashes and charcoal. On removing the stones, some of them crumbled, having been disintegrated by fire. Fireplace No. 4, the diameter of which was six inches greater, contained fifteen inches of ashes and charcoal. Around and beneath the stones of all, the earth had

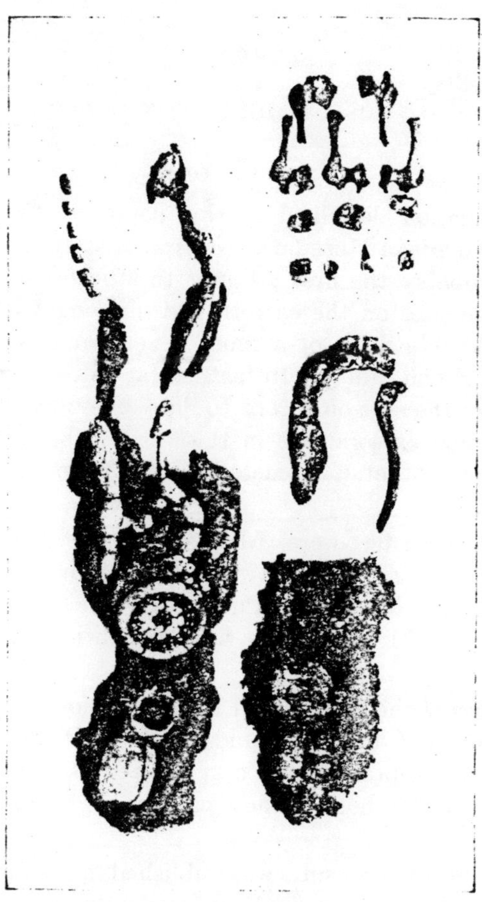

A BAG AND ITS ACCOMPANIMENTS FOUND IN GRAVE 13

been hardened by the fire. No graves were found beyond the northern and eastern limits of the fireplaces.

NOTES

1. William Wallace Tooker. The Indian Place Names on Long Island and Islands Adjacent, with their Probable Significations. New York, 1911, p. 176.
2. Records of the Town of East-Hampton, vol. I, p. 320, Sag Harbor, 1887.
3. Plan of the Town of East-Hampton, 1651. East-Hampton Town Records, vol. II, p. 13.
4. East-Hampton Town Records, vol. I, p. 201 (Book 2, pp. 27, 30–31).
5. Ibid., vol. II, p. 132 (Loose leaf 16–28).
6. James Ward, Historic Ornaments, p. 74. London, 1896.
7. Edwin A. Barber in *American Antiquarian*, vol. II, p. 6.
8. Wilfred Joseph Crips, Old English Plate, p. 279, London, 1914.

AN ANCIENT VILLAGE SITE OF THE SHINNECOCK INDIANS

BY

M. R. HARRINGTON

INTRODUCTION

The investigation described in this paper, carried on under the auspices of the American Museum of Natural History during the summer of 1902, was probably the first attempt to study in detail any of the aboriginal village sites on the eastern end of Long Island, New York, although considerable work of a more general nature had been done before by Tooker[1] and others. In fact, so far as the writer knows, it is the only study of the sort on record to date, the only other publication dealing with actual explorations in this district being a description of the excavation of a Montauk cemetery of the Colonial period[2] and not of a village site.

Assisting the writer were Mr. Arthur C. Parker, now State Archæologist of New York, and Mr. Alanson Skinner, now Curator of Anthropology at the Milwaukee Public Museum. It is interesting to note that this was Mr. Skinner's first expedition and Mr. Parker's second.

The expenses of the first part of the expedition were borne by Mrs. Esther Hermann; but after this fund had become exhausted, Mr. William Weiss of Southampton, New York, assisted us to carry on the work another month; and to both of these patrons the thanks of the Museum are due.

A brief résumé of our results was published in the *Southern Workman* for June, 1903. The work received passing newspaper notice at the time, and in due course a detailed report was made to the Museum. It was not, however, until more than nineteen years had elapsed since our party folded its tents and closed its notebooks for the last time on Shinnecock Hills that the opportunity arrived for the writer to revise his report for publication.

The results of his efforts will be found in the following pages, in which the writer will describe the site, the method of excavation, and the phenomena encountered during the course of the digging. An endeavor will then be made to reconstruct, as nearly as can be done with the scant data which still remain, the material side of the life of the Indians who inhabited this village, and to give a glimpse of their arts and crafts, their dwellings, and the means by which they gained their livelihood.

Fortunately, we are not obliged to depend solely upon the specimens found buried in the earth for our information, although these furnish the bulk of it; for we discovered a few articles of native style still in the hands of the mixed-blood descendants of the Shinnecock Indians who inhabited a nearby settlement at the time of our visit. From these and

---

[1]Tooker, William Wallace. "Some Indian Fishing Stations upon Long Island" (*The Algonquian Series*, New York, 1901).

[2]Saville, Foster H., "A Montauk Cemetery at Easthampton, Long Island" (*Indian Notes and Monographs, Museum of the American Indian, Heye Foundation*, Vol. II, No. 3, New York, 1920).

Reprinted from American Museum of Natural History
ANTHROPOLOGICAL PAPERS, Vol. 22, Pt. 5, 1924.

some of the older whites in the neighborhood was secured considerable information of interest. A knowledge of other tribes of similar culture was found helpful in the interpretation of some of our finds, as were the old records of the town of Southampton, and the accounts of early travelers who met the Long Island and neighboring Indians in their pristine state. These last will be employed by reference only, as Skinner has made full use of them in his accounts,[1] of the Indians about New York City, published by this Museum. Our justification for using the modern Shinnecock artifacts in connection with those exhumed from the ancient village, implying that these also are of Shinnecock origin, will appear later.

Far out, toward the extreme end of Long Island, some eighty miles eastward from New York City, lie the Shinnecock Hills, a rolling sandy tract, almost treeless, but covered with bay and thorn bushes and dotted with little swamps where taller underbrush and even small trees may be seen, rising from a tangle of wild grape vines and wild roses, the blossoms of the former, even more than the latter, filling the air with perfume in late spring and early summer.

The Hills occupy the narrow neck of land between Peconic and Shinnecock bays, the former an arm of Long Island Sound, the latter separated from the Atlantic only by a narrow barrier beach of sand. To the east, the country becomes more level and fertile, and on the Peconic side was still heavily wooded at the time of our visit. On the Atlantic side lies the town of Southampton, even then a popular resort in summer. To the west of Shinnecock Hills the isthmus becomes even narrower, until at Canoe Place but a comparatively few yards of sand divided the waters of Peconic Bay from those of the bay to the south, and consequently, of the Atlantic. Here the Indians had a portage,[1] over which they could drag their canoes a short distance overland from the Atlantic into Long Island Sound by way of Peconic Bay, without being obliged to brave the rough waters in rounding Montauk Point, the extreme eastern tip of the Island, and thereby saving some seventy or eighty miles of distance out and back. The whites also were not slow in appreciating the strategic advantage of the spot with the result that the State has constructed a canal on the site of the old Indian portage for the benefit of local fishermen.

This short cut must have played a considerable part in making the region attractive to the Indian, supplementing its natural advantages of good springs of water, proximity to the ocean and to nearly land-locked bays furnishing the best of fishing and numerous clams and oysters, a nearby forest which must have abounded in game, and convenient fertile tracts suitable for cultivation. In fact, numerous traces of ancient habitation may be seen on every hand, especially on the northern side, where the hills are lower, along the shores and coves of Peconic Bay.

The Site. The largest of these sites, the scene of our investigations, lies along the west bank of Sebonac Creek, which, rising in a series of springs in a little swamp about three-quarters of a mile north of the Shinnecock Hills Golf Club, flows northward for some distance as a fresh water brook. Before long, however, it becomes a tidal creek which in turn broadens out into Bull Head Bay, an arm of Peconic Bay. Scattered along the entire distance from the springs to the bay might be seen patches of decaying oyster and clam shells of varying area and depth,

---

[1]Skinner, Alanson, "The Lenapé Indians of Staten Island" (this series, vol. 3, New York, 1909); "The Indians of Manhattan Island and Vicinity" (*Guide Leaflet Series No. 41, American Museum of Natural History*, New York, 1915).

[1]Tooker, *op. cit.*, 41.

sometimes but a few yards in diameter, sometimes quite extensive. For the most part, these showed on the surface in the form of small fragments of shell only visible to the practised eye among the thin grass and straggling bushes.

To the casual observer such deposits of shells appear to have been laid down on the sea bottom at some time when the present dry land was submerged; in fact, the writer has often been asked if such could not be the case. Upon his reply that the shells were left by the Indians, the questioner almost invariably inquires, "What was their object?" and is usually greatly astonished to learn how simple is the answer: that the aborigines, after gathering the oysters and clams, and bringing them to their village, merely ate them and threw the shells away, and that these shells, accumulating through the years, formed the deposits that have endured until this day.

Ten of these "shell-heaps" were counted on this site, large enough to warrant the conclusion that each represented not one, but a group of ancient habitations, besides smaller ones which probably marked the site of solitary wigwams. They were lettered consecutively on our map as, A, B, C, etc., beginning at the springs and proceeding northward. This map (Fig. 1) shows only five of the shell deposits, however,—those wholly or partially explored—the others lie to the northward, outside of the area represented.

The Excavations

Method of Investigation. Our first procedure in examining one of these deposits was to dig in various parts of it small excavations called test holes, each some eighteen or twenty inches in diameter, penetrating through the shells and other materials composing the "village layer" down to the original undisturbed soil of the site. By "village layer" is meant the accumulated refuse of the Indian village, not only the shells, but the soil blackened by the decay of organic matter, stones shattered and cracked by the heat of ancient campfires, charcoal, ashes, the bones of food animals split for marrow, fragments of broken earthen pots, chips of flint and other refuse from the making of stone implements, and occasional perfect objects of Indian make, lost by accident or hidden for safe-keeping.

By these test holes then, we determined the depth and richness of a deposit, and could then decide what part or parts, if any, warranted more thorough excavation. Should such a place be found the next step was to locate the edge of the deposit and there start a trench running down through the village layer, three or four inches into the undisturbed sand below, and wide enough to allow six feet to each worker. A trench of this kind was carried forward by carefully digging down the front with a trowel, searching the soil for relics, then, with a shovel, throwing the loose earth thus accumulated back out of the way into the part already dug over, so as to expose a new front. Test holes two or three feet deep were sunk into the sand here and there and the digging-down process repeated until the opposite side of the deposit was reached and the indications disappeared. Then another trench was run parallel and adjacent to the first on its richest side, and so on, until the investigator was satisfied that he had covered the entire deposit, or at least as much as his purpose required.

Pits. The object of digging the trenches not merely to the bottom of the village layer, but several inches below it, and of driving test holes, was to detect disturbances running down into the subsoil from the bottom of the deposit. Such disturbances may be very difficult to follow, showing merely slight stains and bits of charcoal running down into the

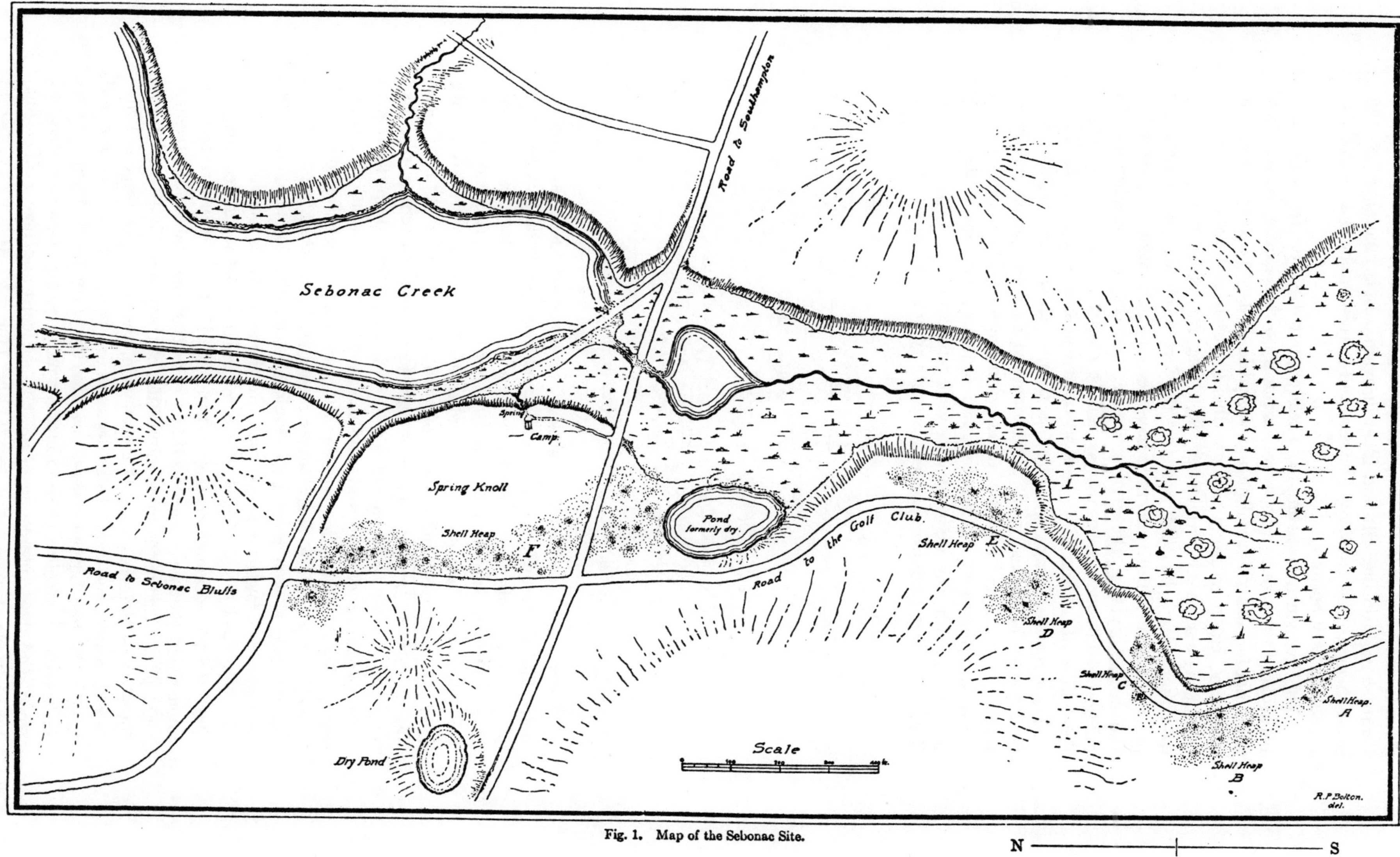

Fig. 1. Map of the Sebonac Site.

N — S

ground; but they indicate that the subsoil at that point had at some distant date been dug out and filled in again. It is incumbent on the archæologist to find out why, if he can, and to this end he must dig them out to the very bottom.

This frequently leads him to a skeleton, but still more frequently the disturbance turns out to be merely a pit, a bowl-shaped or cup-shaped hole, dug for one of several purposes, and later used as a repository for ashes and camp refuse that were thus disposed of neatly and easily. One of the purposes for which they were dug was for the storage of corn over the winter. Probably many of the larger pits were thus first employed, but the majority seem to have been ovens or steaming holes, the Indian prototype of the fireless cooker, and direct progenitor of the modern clambake. As nearly as can be discovered, these holes were lined with stones and a fire built in them which was kept up until hole and stones were piping hot. Then the oysters, clams, meat, or whatever food had to be cooked, were put inside and carefully covered so as to retain the heat, and left until done. Some seem to have been used as cookers, without the addition of stones; others, to have been dug purely and simply for the disposal of odoriferous garbage. The examples described on the following pages illustrate typical forms and sizes.

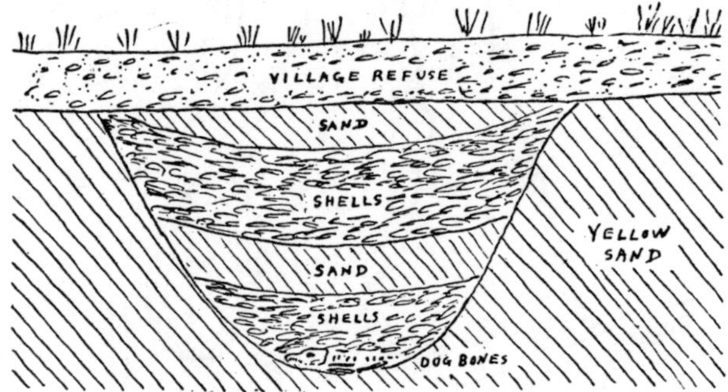

Fig. 2. Section of Pit 62 in Shell-heap A.

Shell-heap A. The first shell-heap examined, designated on our map (Fig. 1) by the letter A, was situated near the little swamp whose springs constitute the source of Sebonac Creek. Numerous test holes dug in different parts revealed the fact that the village layer was shallow, averaging about a foot in depth, and that its groundplan was oval, with a length of 110 feet and a width of about 30 feet. Our tests, although failing to yield prospects good enough to warrant trenching, disclosed one rather unusual pit, about 4 feet wide and 3 feet deep, filled with alternate layers of shells and sand as shown in the section (Fig. 2) and containing disjointed dog bones at the very bottom. Scattered through the other layers were several arrow points and unfinished implements of quartz, two broken bone awls, a piece of deer antler, and numerous animal bones, for the most part split for the marrow, as usual.

Shell-heap B. Shell-heap B was much larger, some 200 feet long by 100 feet wide, although no deeper than Shell-heap A. It proved to be so much richer that we dug no less than twelve trenches, uncovering twenty-eight pits. Among the most interesting of these was Pit 10, which was found to be 53 inches long, 47 inches wide, and 47 inches deep, and contained, besides the usual shells, deer and fish bones, broken pottery, and bone awls, two burned layers, one directly upon the bottom, one six inches above, yielding charred hickory nuts, acorns, bits of rushes and wood, and most interesting of all, charred cord and bits of aboriginal fabric, made of some coarse vegetal fiber (Fig. 3). Another notable pit was No. 28 which was 6 feet in diameter and 4½ feet deep, with a layer of burned shells and ashes in the center. This pit yielded a number of bone awls and worked pieces of antler, an antler arrow point, many fragments of pottery and an unusual number of bones of various animals, birds, and fish, together with a small deposit of still recognizable fish scales in the very bottom. Pit 40 contained, among other objects, thirteen scrapers of quartz and Pit 47, a large mortar stone with two grinding cavities, one on each side.

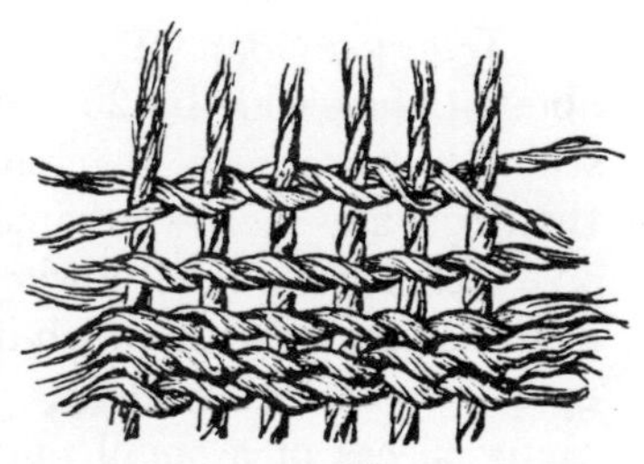

Fig. 3 (20-7472). Piece of Aboriginal Textile.

An unexpected find appeared in Pit 43, which, although but 3 feet wide and 22 inches deep, contained, at 16 inches, the dismembered skeleton of a person some twenty years of age, among whose bones, some of them slightly charred, lay a few bones of an infant. Many potsherds appeared in this pit, some of them lying directly upon the skull. Beneath the bones were found more broken pottery and a number of the bony plates or scales of a large sturgeon. The charring of toes, ankles, pelvis, and ribs suggest that the poor unfortunate may have met death at the stake.

Most instructive of all, however, was Pit 48 which, in spite of its small size (3 feet in diameter and 28 inches deep), yielded an excellent series of specimens illustrating the making of pottery. A lump of unworked clay and some tempered clay lay in the bottom of the pit, while immediately above, fragments of the major portion of a large jar were found. Among the refuse of the pit, which was largely filled with shells of the soft clam, were found two stone pottery smoothers with the clay still adhering (Fig. 4*a*), a bone awl that could have been used to draw the incised designs on a vessel while still soft, a stone muller, probably intended to crush the clay or the tempering materials, probably both, and preserved by accidental burning a small vessel in the course of manufacture showing the coiling process distinctly (Fig. 6).

Among the many arrow-heads, potsherds, and other specimens turned out in the general digging here, one object holds a peculiar interest. It is the perforated circular ornament of claystone shown in Fig. 8, engraved on one side with a figure which suggests the head of a bird (*a*), on the other, with a design which seems to represent an eye, of which the central perforation forms the pupil (*b*).

Shell-heap C. Situated some 100 feet northeast of Shell-heap B lies Shell-heap C, very similar in form to A, but a little larger and a little deeper, averaging 14 inches, as two trenches and a number of test holes showed. A few pits were found here, one of which, a small one, contained a flat pebble, bearing scratched upon it a rude sketch of the face of some animal resembling a lynx (Fig. 7). Much of the ordinary material was found in the general digging, scattered through the whole deposit.

Shell-heap D. On a rise of ground some distance north of the preceding was situated Shell-heap D, which, like it, was of rather small dimensions. It was shallower, measuring only 8 inches, and contained but two pits worthy of the name, one of the common form and contents, the other, Pit 64, more cup-shaped than bowl-shaped, with sides nearly perpendicular. This contained, besides the common bones and sherds, a lynx jaw, a raccoon jaw, and a piece of antler showing cutting.

Shell-heap E. Just east of D, lay Shell-heap E, large and irregular in outline and variable as to depth. This shell-heap was chiefly remarkable because it contained two wigwam sites distinguishable as such, the first the writer had seen in all his three years' archæological digging about New York.

Wigwam Sites. The first wigwam site was an oval of stained earth about 15 feet wide by 20 feet long, and in the center, where the fireplace seems to have been, reaching a depth of 3 feet. The average depth of the floor, however, was some 27 inches. Here were unearthed two massive pieces of a whale's lower jaw bone, still showing at the ends the marks of the stone ax with which it had been cut into lengths (Fig. 5), for what purpose was not evident. Scattered about through the deposit were many pieces of a small pottery vessel, bone awls, and pieces of deer antler showing cutting, besides the ordinary animal bones, flint chips, and the like. Shells and charcoal, while present, were by no means abundant.

Of considerably smaller size was the second wigwam site, which lay about ten feet southeast from the first, for it measured only 10 feet by

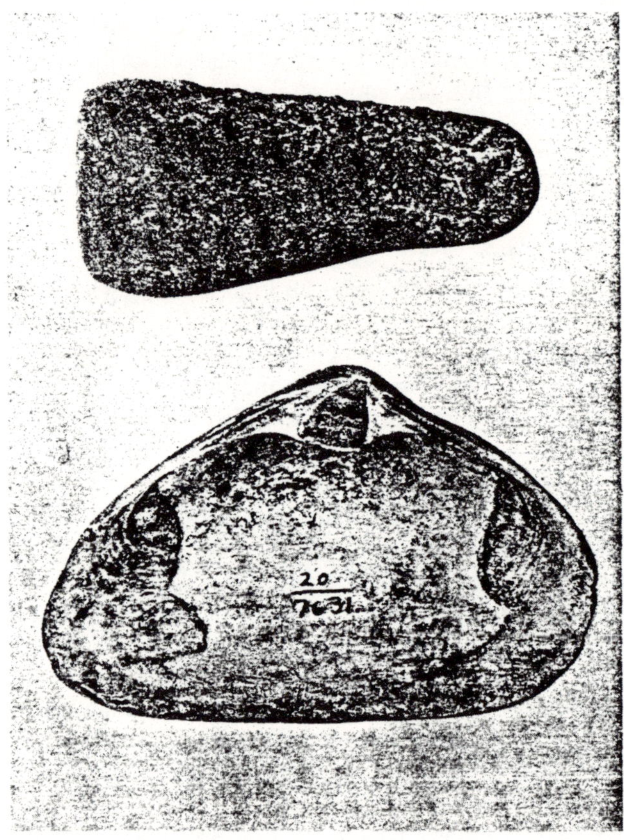

Fig. 4 *ab* (20-7762, 7631). Implements for making Pottery.

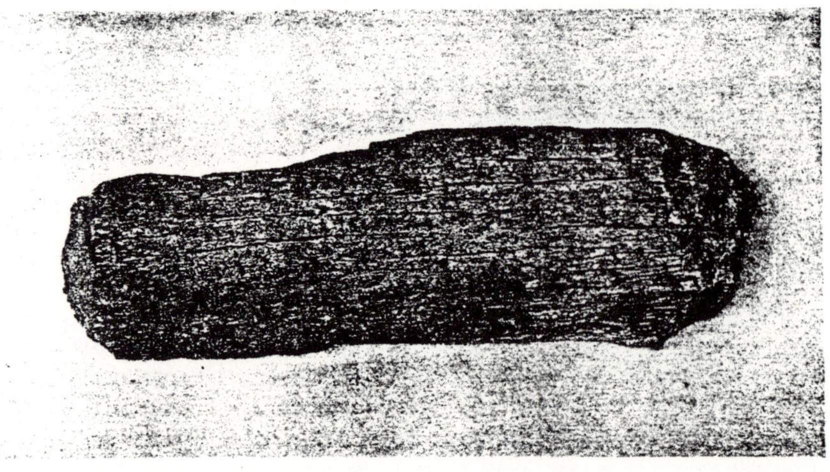

Fig. 5 (20-7918). Piece of Whale's Jawbone showing Marks of the Stone Ax.

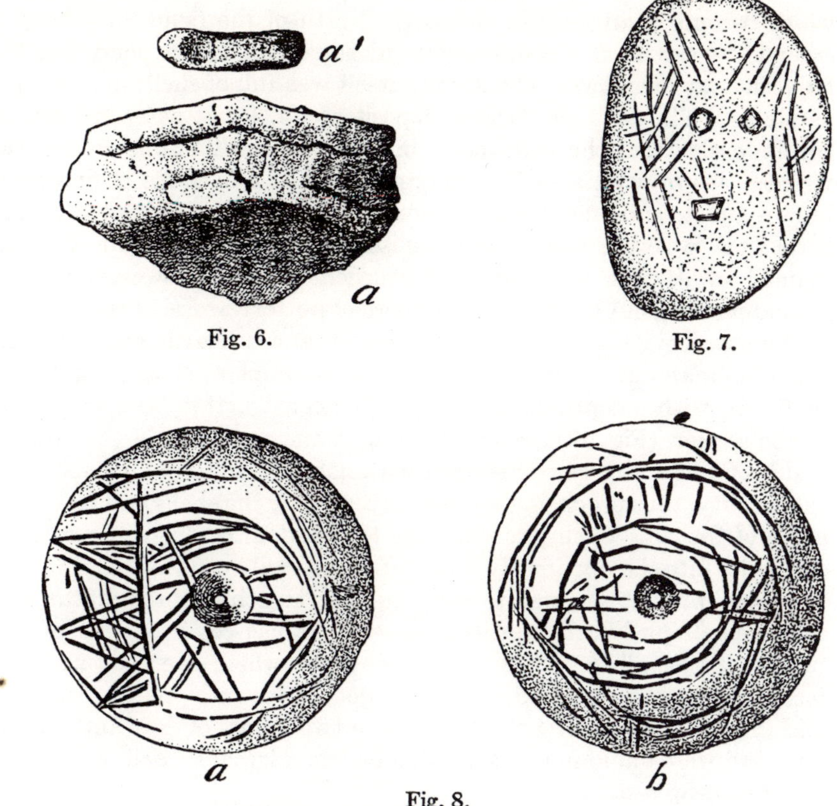

Fig. 6.

Fig. 7.

Fig. 8.

Fig. 6 *a'*, *a* (20-7846, 7774). Part of Pottery Vessel showing Coiling and a Piece of a Clay Coil.

Fig. 7 (20-7627). Pebble showing Drawing of an Animal's Face.

Fig. 8 *ab* (20-7660). Obverse and Reverse of a Clay Stone Pendant showing Designs possibly representing a Bird Head and an Eye, respectively.

15 feet. In the center, where the fireplace had been, was a distinct spot of burned earth, and a deposit of ashes, a little over 2 feet below the present surface. This wigwam site, like the first, was thoroughly excavated, but yielded only the commonest of pottery fragments and split animal bones.

Burial. But a few feet east of the first wigwam site, in Pit 54, a typical burial came to light, the first and only one entirely in anatomical order found on the site. It was the skeleton of an aged person lying flexed on its right side with the head to the southwest, face turned toward the east, and hands near the face (Fig. 9). The only unusual feature was the sunken position of the hips, fully two feet deep, while the head was 14 inches and the feet but 12 inches from the surface. Near the pelvis were two worked stones and a large part of a bowl made from the shell of a box tortoise (Fig. 10). Above and a little south of the knees was a small bed of ashes. Throughout the grave were scattered disintegrating oyster shells, while the skeleton itself was badly decayed.

Copper Bead. This grave had cut into a pit (No. 55) which contained merely the ordinary animal bones and bits of broken pottery, in which respect it resembled several other pits that were opened in the vicinity. A rare article, however, appeared in the northern part of this shell-heap in the general digging, a cylindrical copper bead (Fig. 11), apparently made of the native metal; but without analysis this cannot be stated as a positive fact.

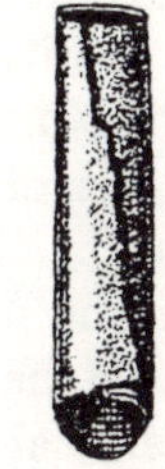

Fig. 11 (20-8026). Copper or Brass Bead.

Shell-heap F. North of Shell-heap E was a small fresh-water pond which became nearly dry in summer. North of the pond Shell-heap F extended down to the swampy ground surrounding the pond and the adjacent salt meadows. The swamp itself was full of shells in a number of places. This was the largest deposit of all, for it extended almost continuously from the little pond in a northerly direction around the western side of what we called the Spring Knoll a distance of five or six hundred feet, and was in places more than a hundred feet wide. The little work we were able to accomplish here in the brief time that remained to us was productive of excellent results, however, for the second pit (No. 59) yielded a nearly perfect pottery vessel of the pointed-bottom variety (Fig. 12), a long bone awl, and a beaver tooth, besides the usual material. This pit was oval in groundplan, measuring 4½ feet by 6 feet, with a depth of 28 inches. The construction, as may be seen in the section (Fig. 13), was rather out of the ordinary, in that the pit had been filled with raw unstained material such as forms the subsoil in the vicinity, thus producing a yellow layer above the shells and blackened earth of the pit. Such pits illustrate the wisdom of digging occasional test holes into the apparently undisturbed subsoil.

This was in the first trench; further trenching brought to light many small pit-like depressions, as well as ash-covered beds of fire-broken stones, all in or below a village layer which averaged about 10 inches deep. This yielded some very good bone awls, many potsherds and the ordinary material. At one place two points of deer antler and a bone awl were found in contact, lying on the original subsoil upon which the shell-heap rests.

Other Deposits. The shell-heaps to the northward toward Peconic Bay, and there were quite a number, were not touched for lack of time.

The Spring Knoll. Between Shell-heap F and Sebonac Creek, at this point expanding into a good-sized salt water cove, is situated the Spring Knoll, one of the most interesting parts of the whole village site. Toward the water, it terminates in a steep cutbank about 10 feet high, extending down to the edge of the creek, where a clear cold spring bubbles forth, while on the land side, beyond the shell-heap, the knoll blends with the brambly, wind-swept Shinnecock Hills. On this knoll, not far from the spring, the explorer's camp was pitched.

Graves. Just south of the crest of the knoll, test holes in one spot revealed dark stains penetrating the yellow sand, with here and there a scattered shell—a likely looking prospect for a grave. We followed these stains, of course, with the result that we soon traced the outline of a pit (No. 11) some five feet in diameter, and shortly afterward, at a depth of 28 inches, encountered the decayed bones of four infants matted together in a compact mass. The pit ran down to a depth of 38 inches and yielded, besides these remains and a few scattered bones of an adult, several fragments of pipes, both earthen and steatite, one of the latter engraved, and the usual sherds, including some fragments of steatite vessels, together with split deer bones and the like.

Pit No. 14, another grave, was found about 10 feet southwest of Pit No. 11. It contained the remains of a child aged about twelve, at a depth of 29 inches to the top of the skull. The skeleton headed east, and lay partly on the stomach with knees northward and feet doubled back to the pelvis. The skull had been displaced and was found facing west near the knees. It was badly cracked and the lower jaw and some of the cervical vertebræ were apparently missing, but were afterwards located near the pelvis. All the other bones were placed naturally. The pit ran down to the depth of 25 inches and contained broken pottery, fish bones, and the like, also a quartz arrow-head.

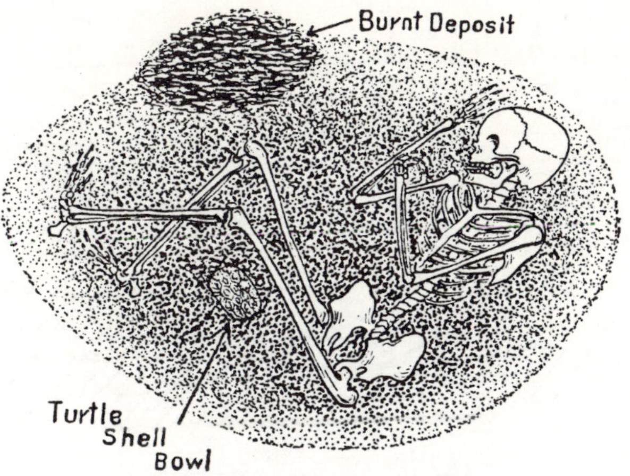

Fig. 9. Sketch of Skeleton in Pit 54.

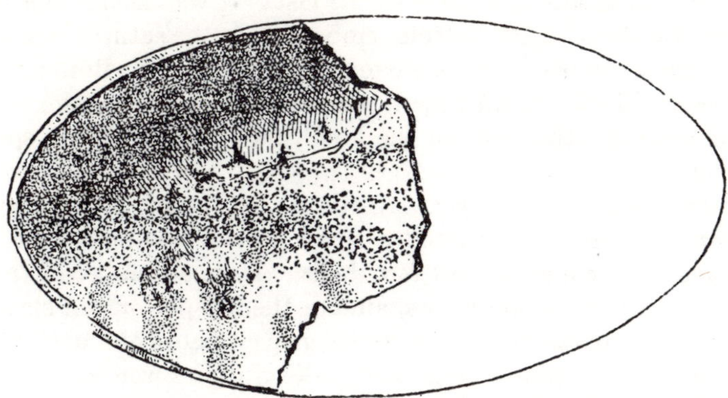

Fig. 10 (20-7937). Part of Tortoise Shell Bowl.

Fig. 12 (20-7975) Pottery Vessel

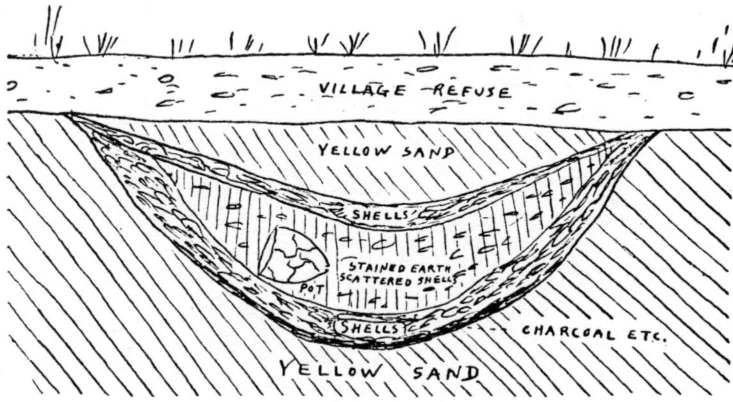

Fig. 13. Section of Pit 59.

Other Pits. Six feet south of Pit No. 14 was Pit No. 35, of unusually large size, being 7 feet wide and 4½ feet deep, a pit which yielded among other material charred corn and cobs. Four feet south was still another pit (No. 36) about the same size as the last. It was nearer the swamp and reached water. In the bottom, embedded in the saturated sand and ashes lay many potsherds and a broken skull and femur. Both articulating surfaces of the femur and the face of the skull were missing. There were a number of other pits on the knoll, but these were not specially interesting.

Spring Knoll Village Layer. North of the summit of the knoll and facing Sebonac Creek is situated a small hollow in which were found many traces of occupation, but few shells. Here a number of trenches brought to light many specimens, among them a perforated clay-stone ornament and a potsherd bearing the engraved figure of a bird, perhaps the mythic "thunderbird" (Fig. 32e). Several pits were exposed here, one of which was Pit No. 1, interesting because it contained near the bottom a large number of land snail shells (*Helix albolabris* and *alternata*) showing the probable use of such snails as food. A section of this pit is shown in Fig. 14.

Archaic Specimens. The soil of the hollow is different from that of the other deposits on this site, as the black village layer reaches the depth of twenty inches in places, with but few and scattered shells. Most of the artifacts were found near the bottom, just above the yellow sand which underlies the whole deposit, but in some cases stemmed arrow points and crude crumbling pottery of a somewhat more archaic character than most of the specimens found here were exhumed from the yellow sand itself. It should be noted, in this connection, that the triangular type of arrow point was the most abundant on this village site; not, however, the narrow triangles associated with Iroquois culture, but the broad form affected by the seaboard Algonkian tribes.

Reconstruction of Shinnecock Culture

Such were the conditions found and such the nature of our excavations. We must now attempt to learn from the specimens exhumed from this ancient village something of the life of its vanished inhabitants, of their means of livelihood, their industries and manufactures, and their relations with other peoples. Only in so far as we may be able to accomplish this will the results of our investigations be of real value. Fortunately, as before mentioned, we have specimens and information gathered from the descendants of this people, old local records, the writings of early travelers, and the surviving practices of similar tribes to help us.

Site identified as Shinnecock. With the exception of the few objects characterized above as archaic, found on and near the top of the sandy subsoil underlying the village layer on the Spring Knoll, all the material found was quite uniform and apparently the work of one people. Some articles made by the whites of the Colonial period (Fig. 15) were found near the surface, indicating that whatever the age of its first settlement the village had been occupied up to the coming of the whites. Now the white settlers found the Shinnecock in full possession of the district;[1] so if the last Indians of the village were Shinnecock, and the deposits for the most part contain the handiwork of only one people, we have good reason for assuming that the village was Shinnecock from first to last. As for the archaic articles, somewhat different in character, found in one spot on the Spring Knoll, these appear to be relics of an earlier camp occupied by a people who may or may not have been the ancestors of the Shinnecock.

Dwellings. What sort of houses stood on the knolls beside Sebonac Creek three hundred years ago? Our excavations told us little, except that they were of oval groundplan, some as small as ten by fifteen feet, some as large as fifteen by twenty feet; that their floors, sometimes at least, were sunk two or three feet below the surrounding surface of the ground; and finally, that the fireplace was in the middle of the floor.

There seemed to be little hope of finding further data. So when we discovered several living people who had seen Shinnecock wigwams in actual use our surprise and pleasure were great. Some of the informants were aged descendants of the Shinnecock; others were elderly whites who had spent their days in the neighborhood; but all agreed on a description which may be stated as follows:—

Poles were bent into intersecting arches until a dome-shaped frame was made from ten to twenty feet in diameter. After all the poles had been tied firmly together, and horizontal strips put in place, the whole was thatched with a species of grass, called "blue vent," put on in overlapping rows, and sewed fast to the strips. When the top was reached, a hole was left open for the escape of smoke, and the edges of the aperture plastered with clay to prevent the thatch from catching fire. The groundplan was circular or oval, sometimes divided into rooms by partitions of wattle-work and thatch. The door frame was an arched pole, the door of wood, or sometimes merely a curtain of skin or mats. An elevated bench or couch of poles generally encircled the interior, beneath which the goods were stored. In at least one case, at a place where poles were difficult to procure, the floor was dug out in the middle so as to leave a shelf around the wall which answered the purpose of bed, seat, and table. The fireplace was in the center.

To preserve this information in tangible form, Mr. W. C. Orchard visited the Shinnecock settlement a few months after our party had left, and under the instruction of Wickam Cuffee (Fig. 35), one of the oldest and purest-blooded of the survivors, prepared a model showing the exact method of construction, which may be seen in Fig. 16. We afterward found a photograph of a full-sized Shinnecock wigwam in the records of the town of Southampton.

Outdoor storehouses were still made in the Shinnecock settlement, at the time of our visit, by digging holes four or five feet deep and roofing them with poles and thatch. One of these may be seen behind the Indian

[1]Thompson, Benjamin Franklin, *History of Long Island from its Discovery and Settlement to the Present Time* (Third edition, revised and greatly enlarged, New York, 1918), vol. 1, 127.

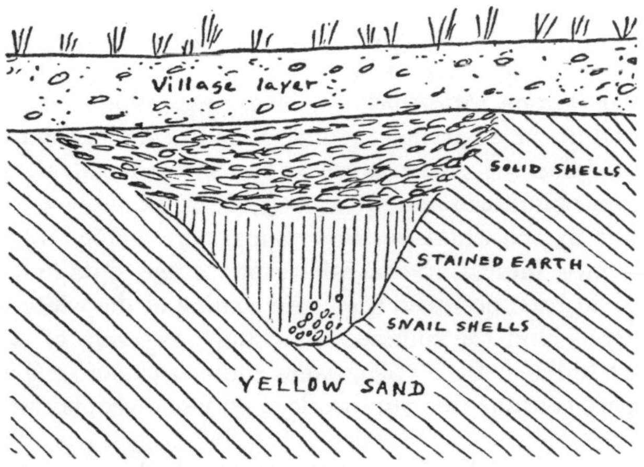

Fig. 14. Section of Pit 1.

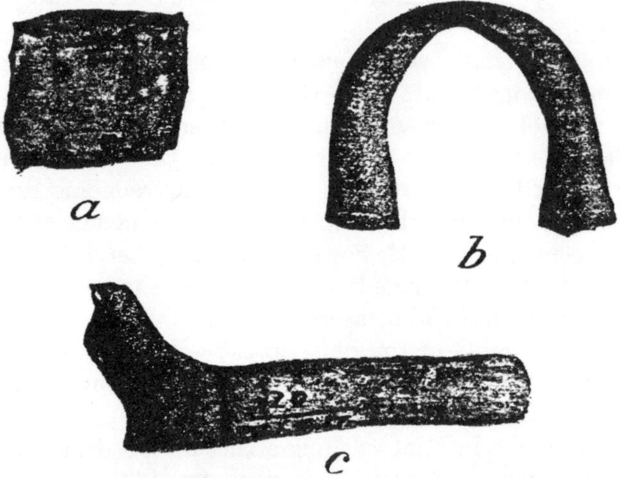

Fig. 15 *abc* (20–7319, 7292, 7667). Objects of European Origin.

Fig. 16 (M–34). Model of Shinnecock Wigwam.

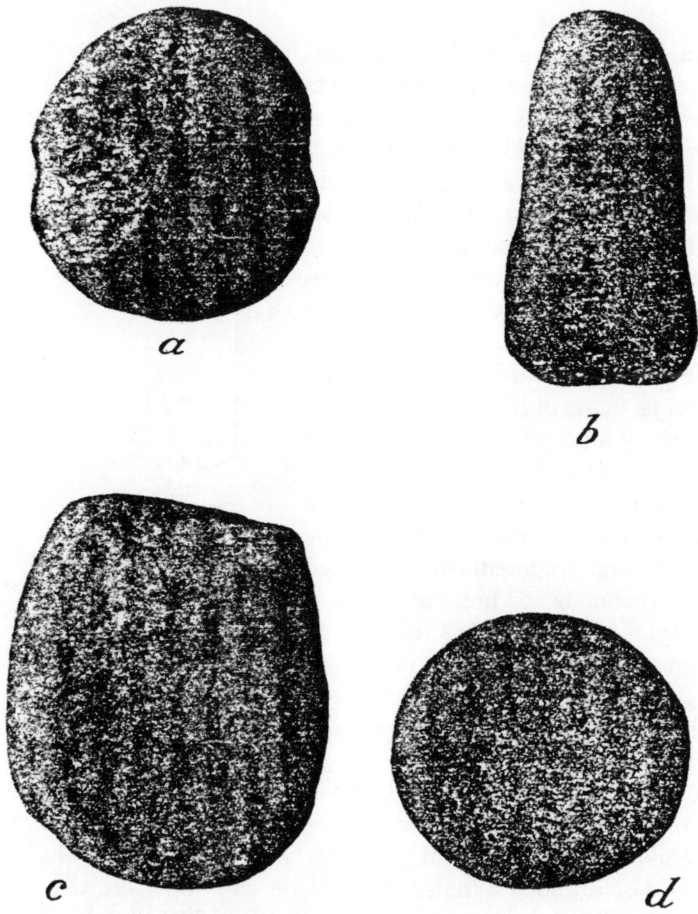

Fig. 17 *a-d* (20–7634, 8000, 7736, 7811). Stone Implements.

in the photograph reproduced in Fig. 38. That this is an ancient method may be established from Colonial records,[1] which mention the "Indian barns" as constituting a danger to the Colonist's cattle, on account of the excavations into which they might fall.

It is, of course, quite possible that the "holes" that gave the good people of Southampton such trouble in 1641 were merely abandoned storage pits that had never been roofed.

Means of Livelihood. A glance at the thousands of rotting shells which compose the bulk of the deposits gives an immediate clue to the outstanding fact of ancient Shinnecock economics: that the sea furnished the greater part of their living. We must not rest content with the idea that oysters, hard clams, soft clams, and scallops constituted the whole of the ocean's contribution, for the refuse layers and pits yielded crumbling bony plates once forming the armor of huge sturgeons, while the teeth of sharks, the bones, and sometimes the scales of other fish, most of them beyond precise identification, together with the claws of crabs, show that the Shinnecock made good use of all the edible creatures the local waters afforded.

As to the method of taking fish, the shell-heaps yielded a few suggestions, among which was the presence of numerous flat pebbles, notched at the edges (Fig. 17a) as if to keep an encircling cord from slipping off. Similar stones may be seen in use as net-sinkers among some tribes

---

[1]Pelletreau, William S., "The First Book of Records of the Town of Southampton with Other Ancient Documents of Historic Value" (*Transcribed with Notes and Introduction*, Sag Harbor, New York, 1874), 22.

today. Such a use for the objects in question is made more probable by historical data referring to the use of nets by nearby peoples.[1] A part of an antler fish hook (Fig. 18a) which, when perfect, probably resembled the bone hook found by Tooker (Fig. 18b), and a slender pointed bone object, so shaped as to suggest its use as a barb for a fish-spear (Fig. 18c), hint at other possible methods, as does the survival, among the neighboring mixed-bloods of today, of fish traps made of basketry of a style once used by most of the tribes of what are now the central Atlantic States.

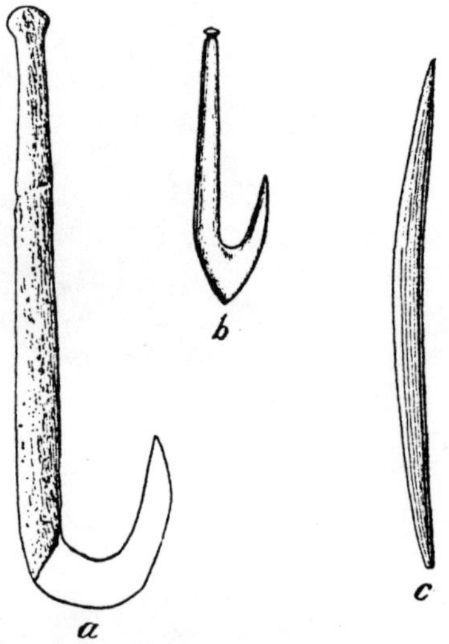

Fig. 18 *a* and *c* (20–7471, 7518), *b* (Tooker Collection). Fish Hooks and Barbs. *a*, Part of antler fish hook; *b*, Bone fish hook; *c*, Bone barb.

We cannot go so far as to state that these Indians actually hunted the whale, although fragments of a barbed antler harpoon head hint at such a possibility. Worked bones of one of these great creatures found in one of the wigwam sites show that they used the whale, whether they harpooned him on the high seas or found him dead on the beach.

Colonial records lead one to believe that they did both, for we find in a deed of April 29, 1648[2] that the Shinnecock, in selling a certain tract retained their hunting and fishing rights, and were to have the "ffynnes and tayles of all such Whales as shall be cast up" on the adjoining beaches; while an ordinance of October 7, 1672[1] "ordered that no Indian employed in the whaling business shall have more than one trucker coat for each whale that his company shall kill, or half the blubber, without the whalebone." Certainly, if Shinnecock "engaged in the whaling business" and their "companies killed whales" only thirty-two years after the coming of the whites, the presumption is strong that they did it before the Colonists arrived, about 1640.

The records of the 1670's are full of contracts in which various Indians agreed to go to sea for certain colonists in pursuit of whales "and other great fish," promised to "use and improve our best skill and strength and utmost endeavor for killing" them, and avowed their intention of taking the best of care of boats and tackle, all for a certain stated payment; with a penalty of so much a day to pay for absence without good excuse.

Certain it is also that in later historic times many Shinnecock shipped as whalers out of Sag Harbor and their seagoing instinct is demonstrated by the tragic fate of twenty-eight of the men, including a large proportion of the full-bloods, who perished while trying to save the stranded ship *Circassian* as late as December 31, 1876.

Although so large a proportion of their food supply came from the sea, quantities of deer bones split for the marrow show that the Shinnecock by no means despised the venison that formed the staple food of so many tribes, while other bones taken from the shell-heaps and pits show that the flesh of the raccoon, muskrat, and even perhaps the lynx, was not neglected, and that due advantage was taken of the spring and fall

---

[1]Van der Donck, Adriaen, "A Description of the New Netherlands" (*Translated from the original Dutch by Hon. Jeremiah Johnson, Collections, New York Historical Society*, 2d series, vol. 1, New York, 1841), 209.
[2]Thompson, *op. cit.*, vol. 2, 87.

[1]*Idem.*, 154.

migrations of wild fowl. Bits of bony carapaces extracted from among the shells of the middens tell of the use of various kinds of turtles as food, and deposits of the shells of land snails would seem to indicate that the primitive Long Islanders were not unfamiliar with that popular French dainty.

The finding of numerous arrow points of stone and of deer antler amid the village refuse and of bones showing wounds, probably made by such points, indicates that shooting with the bow and arrow must have been one of the methods for taking game. All knowledge of other appliances, whether weapons, traps, or snares is now lost. By analogy with styles used by most Eastern tribes, we may surmise that the Shinnecock bow was probably straight, five feet or even more in length, with a rectangular section; and that the arrows were also long, at least thirty inches, and were provided with three feathers. The modern Shinnecock mixed-bloods told the writer that their bow was of hickory, "as long as the man who used it."

The products of agriculture are highly perishable, so it is not surprising that so few cobs and grains of corn or maize appeared in our deposits. The astonishing thing is that some did happen to fall in the fire to be preserved by charring for our instruction hundreds of years later. It is certain, from our knowledge of other eastern tribes, that the raising of corn, beans, and squashes must have been of considerable importance to Shinnecock diet; certainly more than the bare handful of charred cobs and grains would lead us to expect.

Most, if not all, Indian tribes took full advantage of such natural products as their environment afforded in the way of roots, nuts, and berries. The finding of charred hickory nuts leads us to surmise that the Shinnecock were no exception to this general rule. A rather pathetic bit of corroborative evidence appears in the Southampton records[1] where we find that:—

> At a general court held March 6, 1654, it was ordered that noe Indian shall digg for ground nuts on the plain nor in any other ground, upon penalty of sitting in ye stocks for ye first fault, and for the second to be whipped.

Cookery. To describe the cookery of a people after several hundred years have elapsed is no easy task, and cannot, of course, be done in detail. Yet, we are not altogether without clues, for our shell-heaps yielded many potsherds, and a few fragments of steatite vessels, some still so coated with deposits of soot or similar material that we can safely say that liquid foods were boiled in earthen kettles with pointed bottoms, or in oval or rectangular kettles of soapstone provided with handles at the ends, both set directly over the fire. But how could a vessel with pointed bottom be made to stand while the contents was cooking? Such a question naturally suggests itself, but is answered for us by John White of the Roanoke Colony of Virginia, 1585–1588, who made a drawing of a kettle of this type in use, supported by the sticks of firewood, and captioned it "The seething of their meate in Potts of earth."[2] Other tribes who have used pointed-bottom "potts" in recent years frequently support them with three or four stones, between which the point is set.[3]

Now, the question arises as to just what sorts of food were cooked in these vessels. The boiling of meat in the form of soups or stews is suggested by the numerous bones of deer and other animals, which, although split for the marrow fat, considered by most surviving Indians as a great dainty, show no trace of burning or contact with fire at the ends, and so

---

[1] *Idem*, 152.

[2] Holmes, W. H., "Aboriginal Pottery of the Eastern United States" (*Twentieth Annual Report, Bureau of American Ethnology*, Washington, 1903), pl. II.

[3] Skinner, Alanson, "Notes on the Bribri of Costa Rica" (*Indian Notes and Monographs, Museum of the American Indian, Heye Foundation*, vol. 6, no. 3, New York, 1920), 49.

were probably boiled. That some meat at least was roasted or broiled is suggested by the fact that some bones *do* show such burning. The very fact that the burning is mainly confined to the ends indicates that the middle portions were covered with meat at the time of exposure to fire. Tradition among the surviving mixed-blood Shinnecock tells us also that the old people made hominy and "suppawn" or mush from corn, both of which required boiling. Also, that they boiled corn with ashes to remove the hull, washed it free of lye, pounded it in a wooden mortar with a long stone pestle, mixed the resulting meal with berries or beans, according to the season, and finally boiled it in the form of dumplings. Such boiling, in ancient times, meant, of course, the use of the clay or stone pot.

An inspection of the thousands of oyster and clam shells lying about the village site revealed the fact that few, if any, showed any traces of forcible opening, yet seldom were the two valves found together. Comparatively few of them showed traces of fire, so we cannot conclude that they were usually opened by laying them on glowing coals. From these facts, it appears that most of them must have been steamed open, which could best be done in the oven pits of which we found so many examples. From the phenomena we observed in our digging, plus our knowledge of the use of such primitive fireless cookers by other tribes, the method of procedure must have been somewhat as follows: A bowl-shaped hole was dug four or five feet in diameter and two or three feet deep, in which a layer of stones was placed. On these, a good fire was kindled which was kept burning until the stones and the hole itself were piping hot. Then a layer of seaweed was laid in, upon which the shellfish were placed, together with meat or fish, or whatever else the Indians wished to cook. These were covered with more seaweed and earth drawn over the hole to keep in the steam. When the pit was opened some hours later, the shells were all open and the contents ready to eat. Some such arrangement as this was probably the progenitor of the New England clambake, borrowed from the Indians by the colonists.

We found no utensils especially intended for serving food unless the bowls made from the shells of the land tortoise, of which we unearthed a number of fragments, were so employed. The largest piece (Fig. 10) shows that the rim of the carapace had all been cut away and the rib-like bony structures inside scraped out to fit it for use as a bowl. In common with the Mohegan, the Lenapé, and other Eastern Algonkian tribes, the Shinnecock must have used bowls and spoons of wood; in fact we found a few of the latter, resembling the butter ladles of the whites, among the surviving Shinnecock mixed-bloods (Fig. 19c) and early accounts[1] tell of bowls and water vessels made of gourds, some as big as a Dutch bushel, used by neighboring tribes.

Manufactures. An inspection of our collection shows that the ancient Shinnecock employed, as materials for their manufactures, flinty stones, tough stones, soft stones, deer antler, the bones of various animals, shells, clay for pottery making, vegetal fiber for making textiles and cordage, a little copper, and, of course, wood, although we found no actual wooden articles. Arrow points, however, imply arrows of wood. Arrows required bows of wood and the presence of these suggest that other wooden articles must have been used. Such reasoning is not needed, however, for our inquiries concerning woodwork among the modern Shinnecock mixed-bloods brought a number of facts to light, which are doubtless, in part at at least, applicable to the ancient people.

Use of Wood. Wooden mortars of two sizes were in general use: one large, about two feet high, used, with a wooden or a long stone pestle, for preparing corn; the other, small, less than a foot high, in which a

[1]Van der Donck, *op. cit.*, 188.

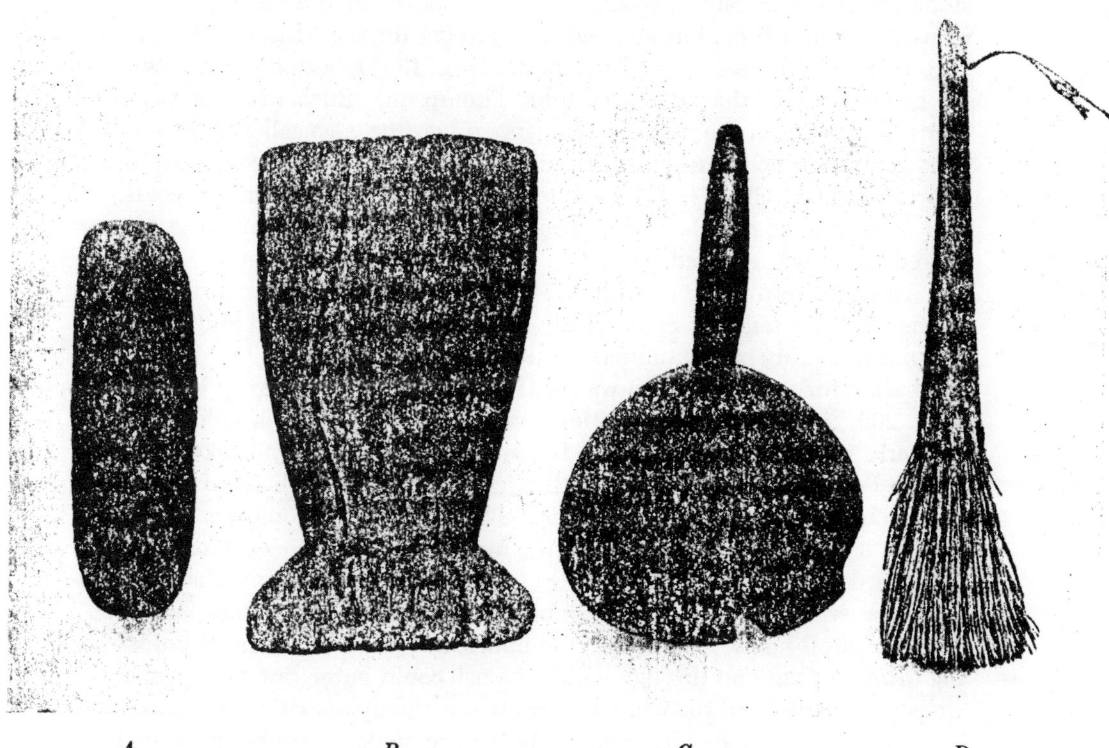

Fig. 19 *a–d* (50–3489b, 3489a 3491, 3494). Modern Shinnecock Implements.

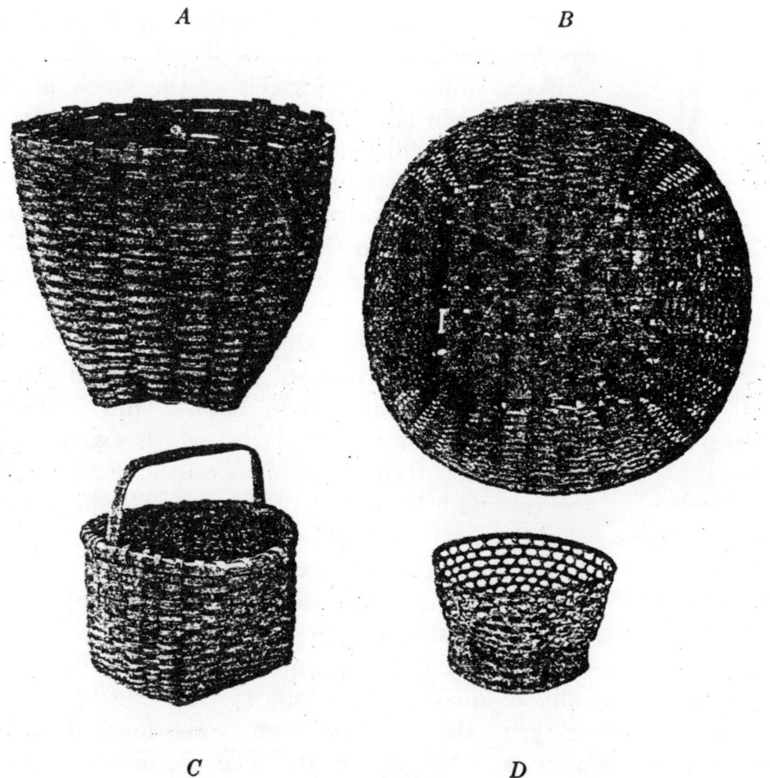

Fig. 20 *a-d* (50–3485, 3483, 3487, 3484). Shinnecock Baskets.

stone pestle was employed to crush herbs. I failed to obtain any specimens of the first type, but succeeded in buying for the Museum the old herb mortar with its original stone pestle (Fig. 19ab), both handed down for generations in the family of John Thompson. Such mortars were made of sections of the trunk of the pepperidge tree, also called tupelo or sour-gum, the wood of which is noted for its toughness and freedom from splitting. The hollows in the mortars were made by laying on live coals and scraping out the charred portion, renewing the coals until the required depth was reached.

Baskets were made of white oak or maple splints in two principal forms, the one tall and cylindrical (Fig. 20a), the other flat and either circular (Fig. 20b) or rectangular in outline, with low sides. The winnowing basket for preparing corn was of the low-sided type. Fancy baskets (Fig. 20d), into whose composition sweetgrass sometimes entered, were formerly made, but this art has become extinct, the only basket now woven being a cylindrical type with a handle (Fig. 20c) identical with a style commonly made by the whites. The splints were sometimes dyed yellow, it is said, by a decoction of the inner bark of a species of oak. A pack basket, carried on the back by means of a band across the forehead was still in common use sixty or seventy years ago for transporting burdens of all kinds. Eel traps of cylindrical form, with a funnel pointing inward at one end through which the fish could enter but not escape, were also made from the white oak splints, a widely distributed type.

Serviceable brushes for cleaning pots were made by splitting the end of a white oak stick into small splints as seen in Fig. 19d and large brooms were sometimes made in the same style. Broad flat wooden ladles (Fig. 19c) were common in old times, many of them resembling the butter ladles of the whites.

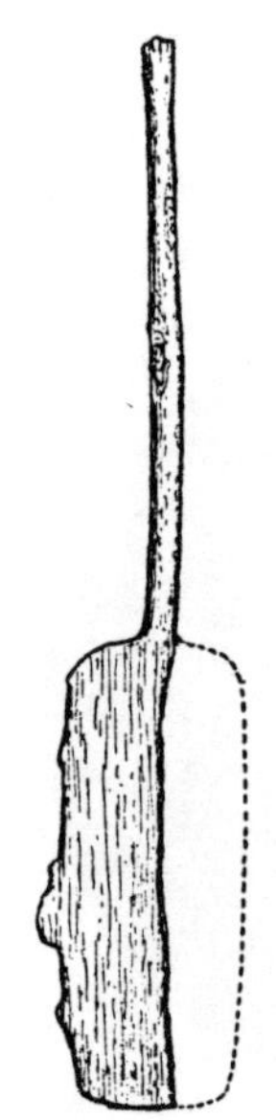

Fig. 21. Ancient Wooden Canoe Paddle. Tooker Collection.

Canoes, it is said, were made of great whitewood or oak logs, hollowed out with the aid of fire, like the wooden mortars. As for paddles, a certain Charles Conklin, while fishing for eels in the creek at Canoe Place, in February, 1880, found the larger part of an ancient oak paddle embedded in the mud. This implement (Fig. 21) measures 34¼ inches long, with a blade which must have originally been at least 8 inches wide. It found its way to the collection of William Wallace Tooker at Sag Harbor, and finally to the Brooklyn Museum.[1]

Stonework. The chipped implements of stone found on the site, probably variously used as arrowheads, spear points, knife blades, and drills, were usually made of white quartz, which exists in abundance in the form of pebbles on the nearby beaches, together with less frequent pebbles of jasper and chert of different colors which were sometimes employed. Argillite was the only exotic material used for chipped implements and this was probably brought in from what is now New Jersey by intertribal trade, already fashioned into implements. The triangular form of arrow point, usually of quartz, as before stated, (Fig. 22a, c), was the predominating type; the stemmed forms were generally, but not always, of other materials (Fig. 22d, e, f). The use of arrow points in hunting has been discussed; that they were also employed in war cannot

[1]Thanks are due to Mr. Foster H. Saville for photographs and information concerning this paddle and other objects in the Tooker Collection. The paddle and the fish hook have been published before. See Tooker, *op. cit.*

be doubted. As may be seen from the typical specimens illustrated (Fig. 22) the arrow points of the Shinnecock are rather irregular in form and crude in finish.

Experiment has shown that the average stone knife was most efficient, not for whittling, but in cutting bone or wood when used as a saw, a process illustrated by many specimens of bone and antler (Fig. 23d) found on this site which have been sawed around with a stone knife and then broken off. Another use of the stone knife was for grooving bones lengthwise until they were divided into long strips suitable for the manufacture of needles or awls. This process is also illustrated by several specimens, and experiment has shown its practicability. Undoubtedly, stone knives were also employed in skinning animals and in cutting meat.

Few drills were found in our excavations, although objects of stone and bone and fragments of pottery showing drilling were not uncommon. Probably the tip of an arrow-head answered all ordinary purposes, especially as, in almost every case, the drilling was done from both sides of the object to be perforated, making a long drill unnecessary.

Chipped scrapers of different kinds were nearly as numerous as arrow points, the sharply bevelled type (Fig. 22h, i) predominating; quartz was the favorite material, or at least the most used, although a few were made of chert and jasper, and one of argillite. Several had been made of broken points re-chipped to give the necessary bevelled edge. Besides their use, noted among other peoples, for cleaning the flesh side of skins from any bits of fat or meat remaining after the preliminary scraping with larger implements, these scrapers were probably employed for scraping down arrow-shafts in much the same manner as the modern carpenter uses a bit of glass, and for shaping and sharpening bone awls,

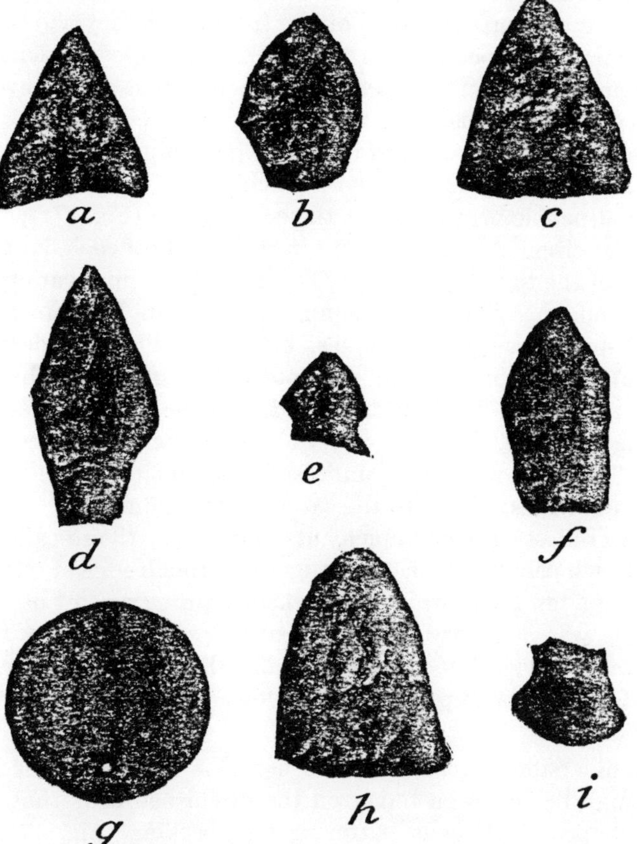

Fig. 22 *a–i* (20–7960, 7990, 7683a, 7857a, 7300, 7837, 7859, 7605, 7465). Chipped Implements and Clay Stone Pendant.

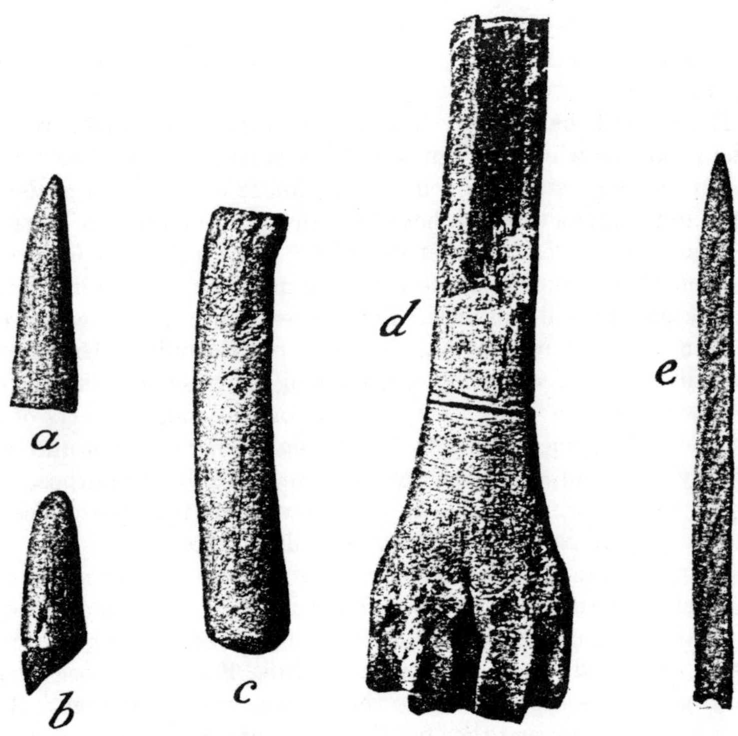

Fig. 23 *a–e* (20–7580, 7580, 7927, 7433, 7544). Objects of Bone and Antler.

which sometimes show distinct traces of this process in the form of slight longitudinal grooves which may be reproduced by experiment.

Large flakes, three or four inches in diameter, usually showing on one side the outer surface of the boulder from which they had been struck, were sometimes chipped so as to produce a disk-shaped implement with a rather blunt edge about the periphery, such as is used by several tribes today in softening skins.

The preliminary flaking in the making of chipped implements seems to have been with hammerstones of which we found two types here: one, the natural pebble bruised about the edge by use (Fig. 17c); the other a more or less circular form with a pit in the middle of each flat side for the reception of the thumb and finger (Fig. 17d), the former variety being the most abundant. Such hammerstones were applied directly to the material in removing large flakes, but punch-like cylinders of antler (Fig. 23c) were probably sometimes interposed between the hammerstone and the edge of the blade to be flaked, and the points were finished by removing fine scales from their edges by pressure with a piece of bone or antler. The large number of unfinished implements, pieces rejected for defects, and flakes, testify to the extent of the industry.

The crudest chipped implements found were the so-called choppers, merely beach pebbles of quartz brought to a rough edge at one end by the removal of a few flakes which fitted them for use as a sort of ax for which no handle was necessary. Sometimes such choppers show the wear of considerable service, but it seems probable that most of them were shaped with a few strokes to serve the need of a moment and were then discarded.

Hammerstones were doubtless used for many purposes, but their effects may be best seen today on the unfinished celts that were being slowly shaped by tedious battering and pecking (Fig. 17b). Broken finished specimens showing careful polishing were unearthed, but no complete examples appeared of this grooveless type of ax, which we know, from complete examples found elsewhere, was mortised into a club-like wooden handle. No examples of the grooved ax, whole or broken, came to light during the digging on the site, but it was probably used by the Shinnecock, unless they differed from most Long Island tribes in this respect, while resembling them in many others. Stone axes of either type were useful in breaking firewood at home and the celt type especially for splitting the skulls of enemies while on the warpath, but were not capable of chopping, as we know the term. For felling trees and cutting them into lengths, it was necessary to apply fire, then to use the stone ax to cut away the charcoal and batter loose the fibers so that the fire might take fresh hold, and repeat the process until the work was done. The marks of a stone ax may be seen on the ends of the large bone (Fig. 5), a relic of a whale cut up by the ancient Shinnecock, mentioned before as found in one of the wigwam sites we explored.

Although we failed to find a good example in our digging, there is no doubt that the ancient Shinnecock used the long cylindrical stone pestle, for a number were found still in use among their mixed-blood descendants who all agreed that the implement formed part of their ancient equipment. Such pestles were undoubtedly made by the same battering and pecking process used in the manufacture of stone axes. The long pestles, as before noted, served to grind corn in deep mortars of pepperidge wood; but that these were not the only pattern used is shown by several shallow mortars of stone found in our excavations. Fig. 26 is a good example, consisting of a stone slab with a cup-shaped hollow on one or both sides. Still another type was a flat slab showing traces of rubbing. Instead of a pestle a water-worn beach pebble was used as a muller with the shallow mortars which may have been employed occasionally to grind corn, but probably served mainly for grinding tempering materials and clay for pottery making, and for crushing dried meat, dried fish, and dried berries.

We have no reason to suppose that the oval steatite vessels provided with lugs at the ends, of which we found several fragments (Fig. 25),

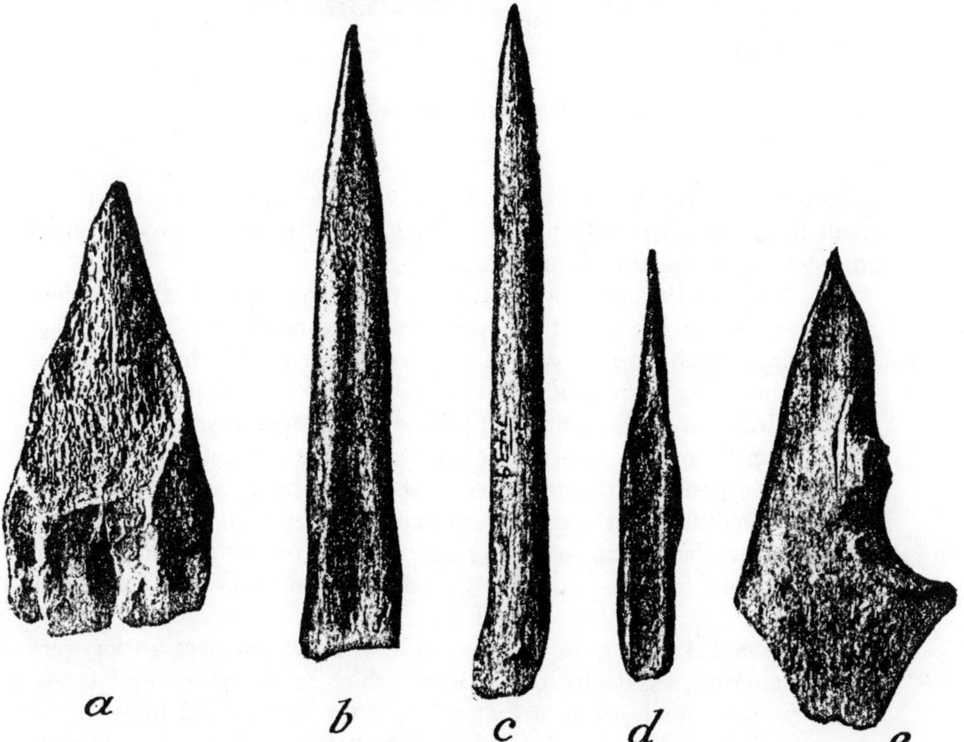

Fig. 24 *a–e* (20–7582, 7535, 7439, 7474, 7622). Bone Awls.

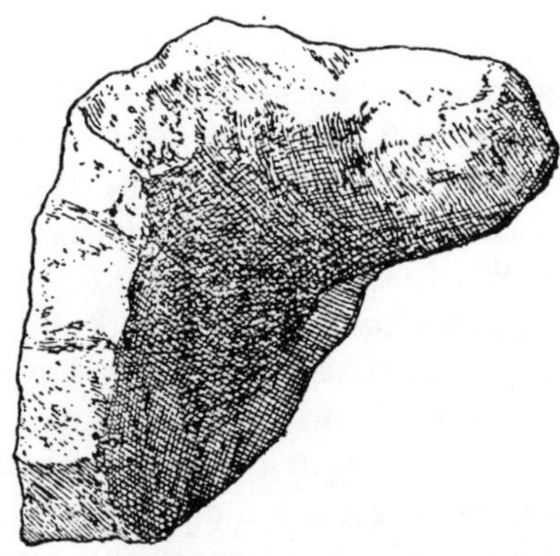

Fig. 25 (20–7492). Fragment of Steatite Vessel showing Handle.

Fig. 26 (20–7757). Stone Mortar.

were made by the Shinnecock. These were probably imported ready made from what is now Connecticut, the nearest point where aboriginal soapstone quarries have been found.

A few small fragments of steatite pipes were found which, when perfect, probably resembled the specimen found nearby by Tooker (Fig. 27), a form which required a separate wooden stem. We have no direct data on how they were made, but the soft stone must have been easily cut and drilled with the usual flint knives and perforators.

The circular pendants made from claystone concretions (Fig. 22g, Fig. 8), one perforated near the edge, the other in the center, could be easily reproduced with similar implements, and the crude design scratched in with a flint point. The scratchings on the specimen shown in Fig. 28 must have been similarly made; it seems to be a fragment of a similar pendant, but of elongated form.

Bone and Antler. Implements made of bone and deer antler were quite numerous, especially the awls, of which we found several types. The best were made from strips cut from the metapodial bone of the deer, carefully rounded and polished (Fig. 24bc). Others were made from the ulna or other large bones of the deer, with the joint left to serve as a handle (Fig. 24ae), but the majority were merely sharpened splinters of bones that had been split open for the marrow (Fig. 24d). The bones of birds or small mammals were more rarely employed in making awls, being too fragile to stand hard service. Most awls were probably used in sewing to make the holes in the skin or other material through which the stiff sinew or fiber thread was thrust. Some were doubtless used in basket making, for sewing sheets of bark together to make trays and buckets, and some perhaps as forks for lifting hot meat from the pot.

Next to the bone awls in point of number were the conical arrow points made from the tips of deer antlers cut off, sharpened, and drilled at the base for the reception of the shaft (Fig. 23a). Sometimes a little projection was left at one side of the hole to serve as a barb (Fig. 23b). That arrow points were also occasionally made of bone is shown by the finding of various fragments, one of which, with a restoration based on the style used by neighboring tribes, may be seen in Fig. 29.

A number of fragmentary bone needles also appeared here (Fig. 23e), made, as in the example illustrated, of bird bone; or more often of a slightly curved strip from a deer's rib; thin and flat, with the eye near the middle, and entirely too broad to use in ordinary sewing. Almost identical needles are still employed among the Central Algonkin tribes, however, for stringing rushes together to make the large mats with which they cover their dome-shaped winter wigwams, so it seems probable that our Shinnecock needles found some similar use. We have historical evidence, to be recounted later, that they used rush mats.

Among the rarer objects were cylinders of antler (Fig. 23c) whose battered ends suggest their use as flint-flaking implements in the manner previously described, a broken harpoon point of deer antler with a perforation and one lateral barb, and a slender barb of bone (Fig. 18c) which may have formed part of a fish spear or may perhaps have been lashed to a wooden shank to form a primitive fishhook, such as is still used among the Montagnais and other tribes. The harpoon cannot be illustrated here, because an important part of it has been lost since finding, but we can state that it had one large lateral barb and was perforated. The use of bowls made of the carapace of the land tortoise, of which numerous fragments (Fig. 10) were found, has been mentioned. That beaver teeth were used for some purpose is assumed from the finding of worked fragments (Fig. 29a). It is known that some tribes had wood-carving tools made of beaver teeth, so perhaps the Shinnecock used them in this way.

The bone implements, complete, broken, and unfinished were studied with some care, and after several attempts had been made to reproduce them in fresh bone with primitive tools, we finally succeeded, and were able to analyze the processes employed. These were sawing, grooving, scraping, grinding, drilling, and polishing. Sawing was accomplished with the edge of a flint knife, a large arrow point, or even with the edge of a large flint flake and was used when it became necessary to cut a piece of bone or antler in two transversely. The edge of the implement was worked to and fro with a saw-like motion against the material until a deep groove was formed. This was continued until it encircled the bone or antler (Fig. 23d) which could then be easily broken in two. Grooving, for the purpose of cutting bone lengthwise, was accomplished with the point of any flint implement or flake. If a strip of bone were needed for the manufacture of an awl, the first step was carefully to mark two parallel longitudinal lines on the surface of the bone selected. These were scratched deeper and deeper with the point of the implement until they became grooves, and finally, until the grooves broke through into the marrow cavity. These slits were connected by a transverse sawing at the ends, whereupon a strip of bone fell out ready for further elabora-

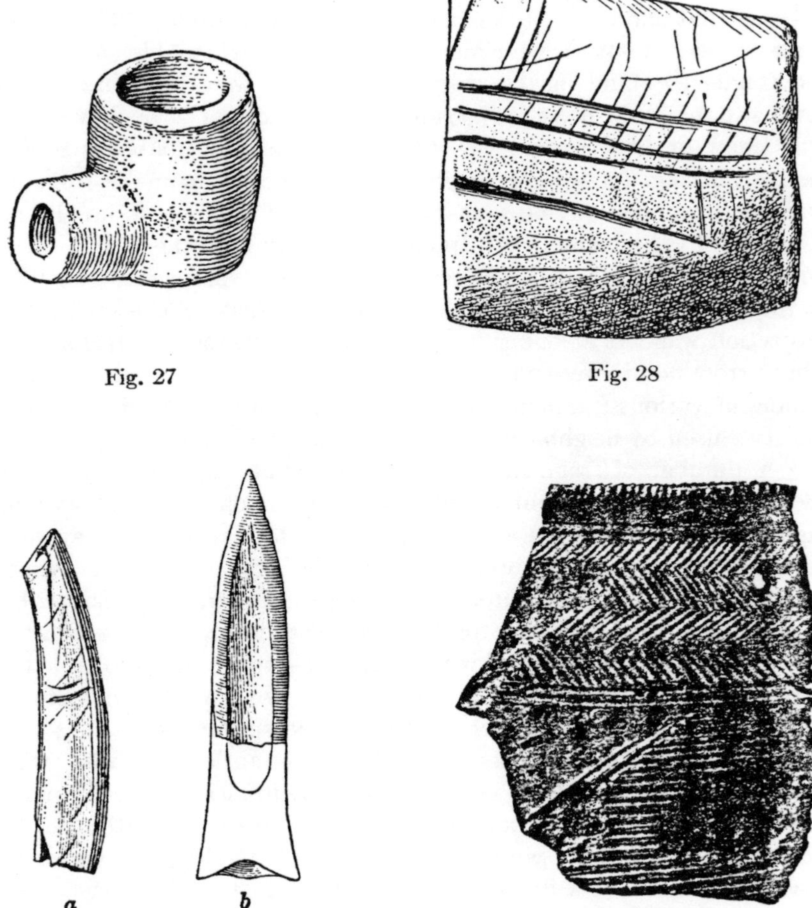

Fig. 27 Fig. 28

Fig. 29 Fig. 30

Fig. 27. Steatite Pipe. Tooker Collection.

Fig. 28 (20–7589). Part of Engraved Stone Pendant.

Fig. 29 *ab* (20–7530, 7553). Worked Beaver Tooth and Restoration of Bone Arrow Point.

Fig. 30 Potsherd, Lenapé Type.

tion. The next step was to scrape off the sharp edges and work out a rough point with a bevelled edge scraper, or even a flint chip, used much as a modern carpenter scrapes wood with a piece of glass; then a gritty stone was employed to grind it into final shape. The marks of this grinding may be seen on the awl (Fig. 24b). The final polish was then put on by rubbing with the smooth surface of a beach-pebble. The eyes of the broad bone needles can easily be reproduced with the point of an arrowhead rotated after the manner of a drill, first on one side of the needle until partly bored through, then on the other. Since the cavities in the bases of antler arrow points for the reception of the shaft were deeper they had to be bored with a narrow flint drill which worked best, as experiment shows, attached to a short wooden handle.

Pottery. One nearly complete pottery vessel was secured (Fig. 12) and enough parts of another to restore its form, together with many fragments, all of which served to show that the typical ancient Shinnecock pot was somewhat egg-shaped, with pointed base and slightly expanded mouth, of the archaic Algonkin type found all along the Atlantic Coast from Virginia to Maine.[1] This type was, however, modified about the mouth of the Hudson and in New England by Iroquian influence which

---

[1]Holmes, *op. cit.*, 150–158, 175–179.

seems to have first made itself felt shortly before the coming of the whites. In capacity, these vessels seem to have varied from about six quarts to perhaps four or five gallons. That they were used directly on the fire may be seen by the smoked and blackened condition of some of the bottoms. Sometimes, when cracked, they were repaired by boring a series of holes in pairs on opposite sides of the split and then lacing it together, probably with thongs. Such repaired vessels could not very well have been used in cooking, but they must have made good water jars when properly pitched to prevent leakage.

In one pit, we were lucky enough to find the greater part of a potter's outfit, which shed considerable light on the Shinnecock method of making earthenware. The first stage was illustrated by a lump of raw clay and some clay thoroughly mixed with the crushed shells here often used as tempering material; the second, by pieces of clay coils and part of a small unfinished vessel (Fig. 6), all preserved by accidental burning, which showed that the clay had been worked out into long rolls with which the vessel was then built up, coil on coil, the coils being smoothed and blended as the work proceeded. The pit even yielded some tools with which the blending was done, in the shape of two beach pebbles showing wear and still daubed with clay (Fig. 4a). In other parts of the site were found clay-covered shells of the "hen clam," the worn edges of which showed long use for such purposes (Fig. 4b).

Some years after these excavations were made, the author had occasion to visit the Indians of South Carolina, where the making of pottery by aboriginal methods was found to be a still living industry. I was interested then to observe that the Catawba used the coil method, blending the coils with smooth pebbles kept constantly wet, and with fresh-water clam shells which showed wear in exactly the same place as the "hen-clam" pottery scrapers we had found on Shinnecock Hills. After completing the vessels the Catawba dried them a few days in the shade and then arranged them around a brisk fire, mouth to the blaze.

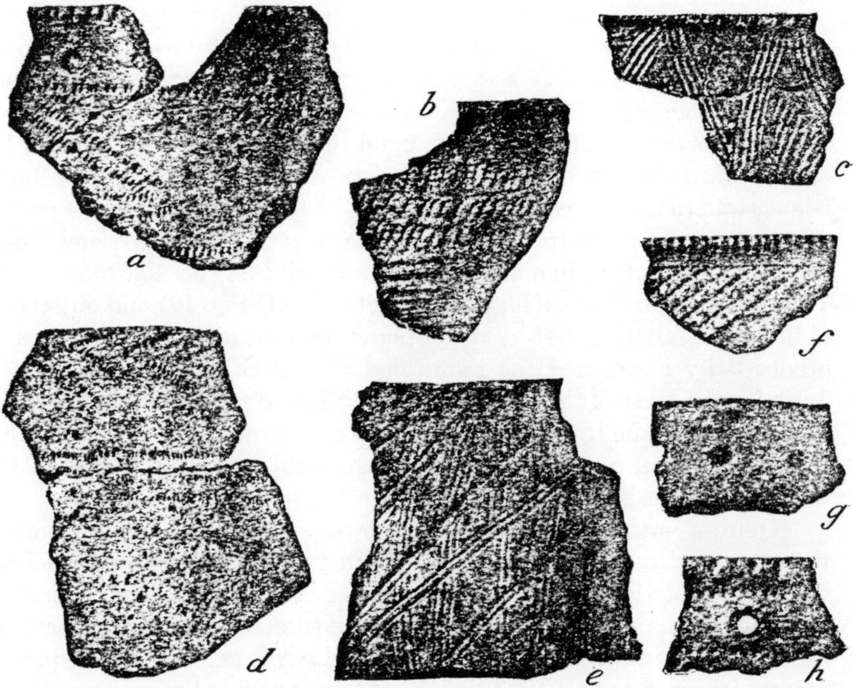

Fig. 31 *a–h* (20–7985, 7935, 7810, 7985, 7598,-7985, 7967, 7847). Potsherds showing Decoration.

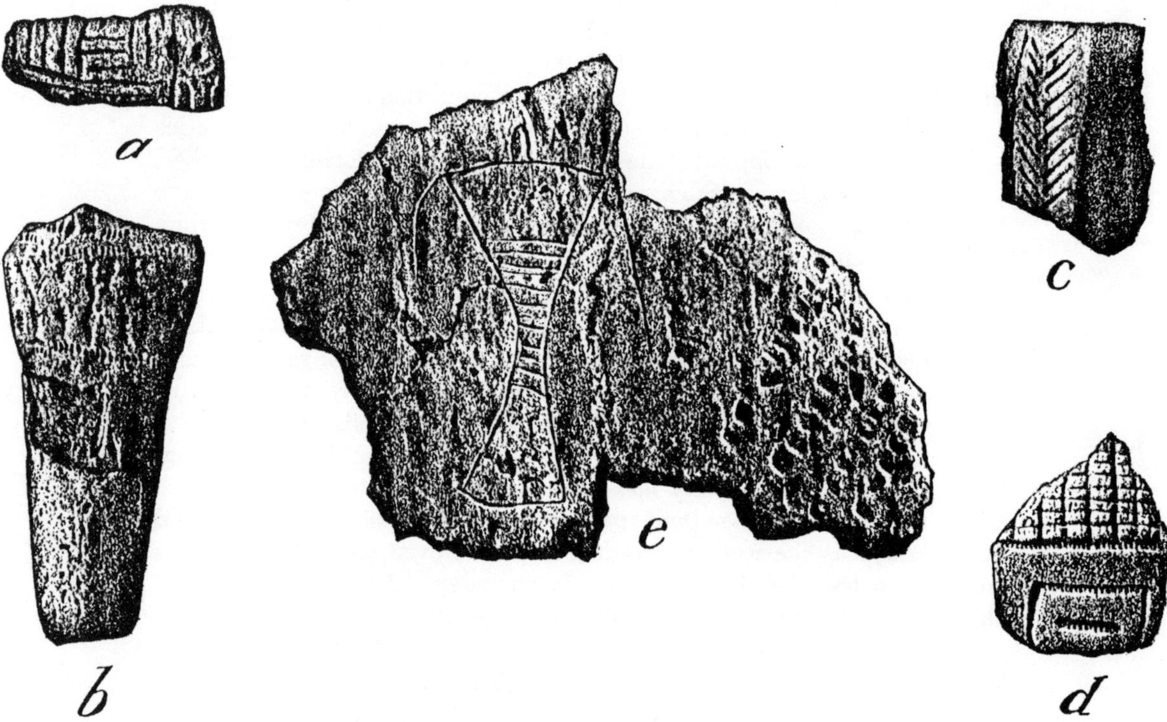

Fig. 32 *a–e* (20–7920, 7453, 7293, 7451, 7829). Pipe Fragments and Potsherd bearing Sketch of Bird.

After a while, they assumed a darker color, and when this had become uniform, a sign the vessels were hot enough, the blazing brands were raked out of the fire, the vessels inverted over the coals and hot ashes which were pushed up around them, and the whole covered thickly with pieces of dry bark pulled from old pine stumps. When the bark had burned away the red-hot vessels were pulled out and allowed to cool around the smouldering embers.[1] Probably the ancient Shinnecock dried and fired their pottery in a somewhat similar manner.

The decoration of Shinnecock ware was effected while the clay was still fairly soft. The crude patterns were produced by several methods, one of them the ordinary one of incising with a sharp point, possibly that of a bone awl (Fig. 31f, Fig. 30). Another method was to wrap a twig in fiber twine and impress this upon the plastic clay (Fig. 31*a*, *d*, *h*), while a third, which seems characteristic of the eastern end of Long Island, was to drag a section of the edge of a scallop shell along in such a manner as to produce from two to six parallel grooves, and sometimes, instead of dragging it, to make successive imprints of the edge of the shell. This method may be seen on the complete vessel (Fig. 12) and on several of the fragments (Fig. 31*b*, *c*, *e*). A punctate form of decoration was also produced by imprinting the round end of a stick (Fig. 31a, g, h). A finish for the body of the vessel was often applied with a paddle wrapped in fiber cord, while the inner surface was sometimes marked by scraping with the edge of a stone serrated by chipping, as was one side of the smoothing stone shown in Fig. 4a.

Quite a number of fragmentary pottery pipes were found, some of them nicely decorated, as may be seen in Fig. 32. These differed from the stone pipes found in this region by Tooker (Fig. 27) and others in that they were provided with a short stem, sometimes round, sometimes flat in section, made in one piece with the bowl, and did not require a separate wooden stem. How they must have appeared when complete is

---

[1]Harrington, M. R., "Catawba Potters and their Work" (*American Anthropologist*, N. S., vol. 10, pp. 399–418, 1908).

shown by the perfect specimen (Fig. 34) found at Canoe Place, and now in the Museum of the American Indian, Heye Foundation, as the gift of the Long Island Historical Society.

Weaving. That the Shinnecock, in common with most of the Eastern Algonkian tribes made numerous rush mats and wove a variety of sacks and bags, burden straps, and perhaps even garters, belts, and garments out of fiber cannot be doubted; but the only specimens we found to prove it were a few fragments of native cloth preserved by charring (Fig. 3). Noticeable features were the coarseness of the fiber composing the cord of which the fabric was woven, and the fact that the weft threads were run in pairs with a twist together between every strand of the warp, a simple form of the twined weave so characteristic of aboriginal textiles in most parts of North America where any weaving was done at all.

We can prove, as before stated, the use of mats among the Shinnecock and neighboring Indians by several historical references; for instance, in the agreement between Lion Gardiner and the Indians[1] in which he grants them "liberty to cut in the summer time flags, bull-rushes and such things as they make their mats of" on a certain tract "provided they do no hurt to the horses" pastured there.

Art and Ornament. The decorative art of the Shinnecock, as shown in wood carving, in the painting of designs on various objects, and in whatever form of embroidery they may have used (probably with dyed deer hair) has been lost beyond recovery. All that remains for us to study are their pottery decorations on vessels and pipes, and a few markings on stone and wood. The story is soon told, for the former are of the simplest. Most abundant are combinations of straight lines forming bands parallel to the rim of the vessel, combined with angles or chevrons which may point horizontally (Fig. 31a, d), or vertically (Fig. 31c). Sometimes lines singly or in parallel groups may run vertically, instead of horizontally, or may be placed diagonally, as may be seen in the whole vessel (Fig. 12), and in the potsherd (Fig. 31e), and cross-hatch patterns sometimes appear (Fig. 31f).

These designs, as before noted, were usually produced by the imprints of cord-wrapped twigs (Fig. 31a, d, h); by groups of parallel lines drawn with pieces of the edges of scallop or mussel shells (Fig. 31c, e, Fig. 12); by imprints of the edges of such shells (Fig. 33b, Fig. 12); and by marks and notches made with the point of a sharp instrument such as a bone awl (Fig. 31f). The lines and angles are often interspersed with circular imprints of the end of some blunt cylindrical instrument (Fig. 31 a, g, h).

The decoration of most of the pottery was exceedingly crude, with no attempt at color work, no curved lines, and with a very few exceptions, no attempt was made at elaborate patterns even in straight lines and angles. There was one exceptional sherd, however, that showed a tasteful, well-executed, and fairly complex pattern (Fig. 30), consisting of a band of closely set chevrons forming a herring-bone design surmounting a band of large triangles filled with parallel horizontal lines and pointing upward, the spaces between them being left plain. This, however, is so divergent from Long Island pottery in general, and resembles so closely the Lenapé ware found near Trenton, New Jersey,[1] that the chances are that it was obtained in trade from that region and was not of Shinnecock manufacture at all. The sherd shown in Fig. 31f may also belong in the same category.

---

[1]Southampton Records, *op. cit.*, 170.

[1]Volk, Ernest, "The Archæology of the Delaware Valley" (*Papers, Peabody Museum of American Archæology and Ethnology*, vol. 5, 1911), pls. CXII, CXIII, CXIV.

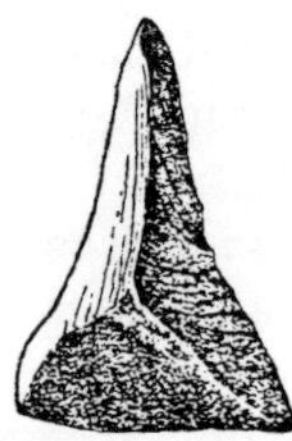
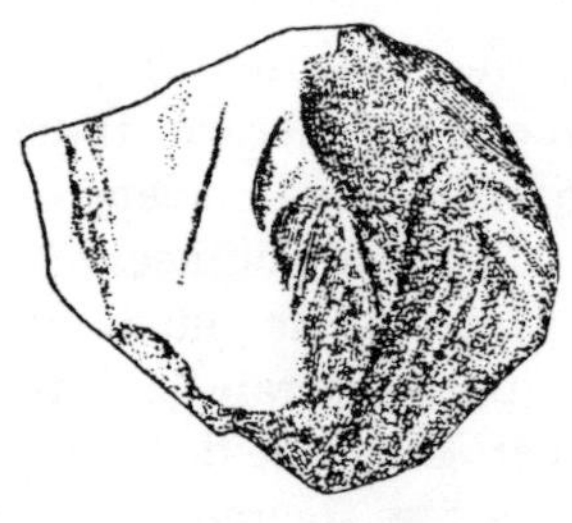

Fig. 33 *ab* (20–8036, 7779). Black and Red Paint Stones, Graphite and Limonite, respectively.

The designs just described are all of a purely geometric character; we did find, however, a few attempts at realistic ornament. One of these is the crude drawing of a bird scratched on a stray potsherd (Fig. 32e), an hourglass-shaped figure whose head is represented by a slight projection and the wings by drooping lines. It is particularly interesting on account of its practical identity with drawings still made by the Central Algonkin tribes and their neighbors to represent a Thunderbird, a race of mythic beings who were thought to be the patrons of warriors, the bringers of rain for the crops, and the guardians of mankind against water monsters.

Perhaps also connected with tribal tradition are the rough sketch of the head of some animal, possibly a lynx, engraved on one side of a pebble (Fig. 7); while a slight stretch of the imagination might interpret the markings on one side of the circular gorget seen in Fig. 8a as the profile of a turkey, while those on the reverse side may represent a human eye (Fig. 8b).

We found little to indicate personal decoration, except the circular gorgets or pendants (Fig. 22g, Fig. 8), a coarse shell bead, since lost, and the copper bead (Fig. 11) which may be made of native metal. The

Fig. 34. Earthen Pipe, Canoe Place. Courtesy of the Museum of the American Indian, Heye Foundation.

paint, red and black, ground from deeply scored bits of limonite (Fig. 33b) and graphite (Fig. 33a) was probably, for the most part, applied to the faces of the Shinnecock.

Trade. As previously noted, the presence of implements made of purple argillite in the refuse deposits indicates trade with the tribes of New Jersey, as does the appearance of a few sherds of typical Trenton Lenapé pottery; fragments of steatite cooking vessels and pipes show commerce with Connecticut tribes (the nearest quarries were there), while a number of objects, all found in the upper layers of the deposits, bear witness to the latter day trade with the whites. Examples of these are shown in Fig. 15 and consist of a gun flint (*a*), the handle of a brass kettle (*b*), and part of a trade pipe of clay (*c*).

If the copper bead, which, as may be seen from the drawing (Fig. 11) has been made by rolling a flat bit of the metal into cylindrical form, should prove on analysis to have been made from a native nugget, intertribal trade from so distant a region as Lake Superior would be estab-

Fig. 35. Portrait of Wickam Cuffee.

lished. If not, we have merely another specimen showing trade with Europeans.

Fate of the Shinnecock. The Shinnecock truly sold "their birthright for a mess of pottage" in 1640 when they placed their marks as signatures on the first deed to the English settlers. From that time onward, the town records of Southampton[1] are our best source for learning what befell them. We find many early town ordinances that must have proved irritating in the extreme, for example, the one before quoted, forbidding the Indians to dig for ground nuts. We observe also that they were at first not permitted in the town at all, that no one was allowed to sell them food; and perhaps most onerous of all, that they were ordered to kill their dogs. No wonder they were sometimes rebellious, and once attacked Southampton and burned several houses, for which damage they were later compelled to pay.

On the other hand, we find that it was lawful to sell food to the sachem for his own use, but to no one else, and in another place it was made lawful to sell an Indian flour, provided it was of the coarsest quality. In 1649 it was permitted to the Indian women to come to town on shopping tours, and then the same privilege was extended to the "ancient men" to do the same, but these must first obtain "tickets." Still more considerate was an ordinance forbidding the whites to turn out their

[1]Southampton Records, *op. cit.*

Fig. 36. Portrait of Charles S. Bunn.

Fig. 37. Portrait of Mrs. A. E. Waters

"Hoggs or piggs" on the Indians' land, that their corn be not damaged, and another in 1653 providing that "if the Indians will suitably fence one half between them and us that then ye towne will fence the other half." By 1675 the relations of the two races had so improved that many Indians were employed by the whites to go to sea for them in pursuit of whales.

Of the Shinnecock's relations with other Indians we learn of their distress on account of a threatened attack by "Naragansets" in 1653, and of their submission to Wyandance of Montauk, whom they acknowledged as "Sachem of Pawmanack or Long Island." He however was brother of their own chief, Nowedonah.

Little record was made of the Shinnecock after they ceased to be, from the settler's point of view, a menace to the colony, and took their place in its whaling and other industries. We learn from other sources[2] that many of them went to Brotherton, in Oneida County, New York, about 1789, where they joined the remnants of various New England tribes, and in 1833 moved with them to Wisconsin, where their mixed descendants may still be found.

Some of those left behind intermarried with negroes, a phenomenon seen among several remnants of Atlantic Coast tribes and among some Muskhogean peoples, but exceedingly rare elsewhere, fortunately for the future of the Indian race. Certain it is that the African mixture has lost for the Long Island survivors the respect and support of the Iroquois tribes who now will not recognize them in any way, and will not even admit that there is any Indian blood left on Long Island.

There has been a heavy infusion of white blood too, but affairs had progressed so far that when I paid my first visit to the Shinnecock "Reservation," in 1902, the place appeared to be a negro, or rather, mulatto settlement, pure and simple. But more careful search revealed a number

[2]"Handbook of American Indians" (*Bulletin 30, Bureau of American Ethnology*, Washington, 1907, 1910), part 1, 166; part 2, 550.

Fig. 38.

Fig. 39.

Fig. 38. Portrait of John H. Thompson.
Fig. 39. Portrait of Mary Ann Cuffee.

of individuals showing Indian characteristics. To quote my notes, written at the time:—

Some are black and woolly headed, having at the same time facial characteristics distinctly Indian. Others have the straight hair and light color of the Indian, but the flat nose, large dull eyes, and thick lips of the negro. A few of the men are typically Indian. Of these, Wickam Cuffee (Fig. 35) is the best example. He is Indian in color and feature, and claims to be full blooded, but the slight curl in his hair seems to point to some admixture. He speaks with a Yankee accent, and gladly tells all he knows of the old times. Andrew Cuffee, the blind ex-whaler, also presents many Indian characteristics, while Charles Bunn, Fig. 36, (with a slight tinge of negro) and John Thompson (Fig. 38) (part white) are good types. Very few of the young men on the reserve show Indian characteristics. A number of the women are pure or nearly pure-blooded Indian Among them are Mary Brewer, Mary Ann Cuffee (Fig. 39) and Mrs. Waters (Fig. 37). The preponderance of women over men is accounted for by the drowning of most of the Indian men when the ship *Circassian,* stranded off Easthampton, was destroyed, on December 31, 1876, by a sudden storm. Then it was that the corpses of the Shinnecock salvers, each incased in a mass of frozen sand, were found scattered along the bleak ocean beach from Amagansett to Montauk. Thus perished the flower of the tribe—the expert whalers who had sailed on many successful voyages out of Sag Harbor or New Bedford— the men whom their white neighbors still speak of as being "noble-looking, strong, and tall."

Many of the survivors, especially the younger ones, have left the reservation, and are now scattered abroad. The only Indian children seen during my entire stay were visitors from Shinnecock families settled elsewhere.[1]

That such survivors still exist and still show strong Indian characteristics without visible African admixture is proved by a photograph recently taken at Easthampton which was published in the *New York Evening Post,* March 18, 1922. Very likely the destruction of the "flower of the tribe" in 1876 left the negroid mixed-bloods in the majority in the settlement, which was so distasteful to the remaining Indian families that all who were financially able moved away.

Cultural and Linguistic Position

Our investigations, so far as they went, show that the Shinnecock were, in a general way, similar in material culture to the other tribes of Long Island and the coast of the adjoining mainland. However, they differed in some particulars from the tribes at the western tip of Long Island and elsewhere in the immediate vicinity of New York City, for which region we possess considerable data.

English	Shinnecock	Natick	Narragansett	Abnaki (St. Francis)	Malecite	Delaware	Sauk
turtle	matci'k				miktcik = tortoise		meci'käha
snake	skuk	askook	askùs	skuks		achgook	
man	tcais[1]	kehchis = old man	chise = old man				
woman	wi'nai[1]		wenȳgh				
woman	skwa	squaas	squàws	skwa		ochqueu	i'kwäwa
child	papús	papeissesu = little one	papoos				
sea-beach	siwáa	sée = sour		siwán = salt		schewewah = salt	
rain	kĕ'mĭo				kemi'wan		kĕmiyawĭ
house	wĭ'kam	week = his house		wĭkóm			wikĭyapĭ
corn mush	suppâ'n	saupáun = softened				{sachsapan = soup; sä'pan = mush}	
shellfish	sĕ'tcawa		sucksawaug = clams (Pequot)				
thanks!	tabŭtni'	tabuttantam— he is thankful	taubut neanawáyean = I thank you				
greeting!	hah'cami						hau!
come quick!	mĕkwi'		muckquetu— he is swift				

[1]The words ktcais, husband, old man; and wĭnai's, wife, old woman, occur in the Mohegan dialect spoken until recently in Connecticut; Speck, Frank G., "Notes on the Mohegan and Niantic Indians" (This series, vol. 3, 1909), 194.
"Chice" appears in the Southampton records as the name of a Shinnecock sachem.

[1]Harrington, M. R., "Shinnecock Notes" (*Journal of American Folk-Lore,* vol. 16, 1903), 37–39.

For instance, the Shinnecock seem to have used the dome-shaped, thatched wigwam in preference to all other types, a variety not mentioned by early travelers about New Amsterdam; also, their pottery, although similar in form to the archaic ware of western Long Island, differs from it in the more abundant use of pounded shells for tempering the clay, and in certain decorations. Moreover, the Shinnecock made little use of the grooved ax, so popular among the Rockaway and Canarsie, and used many more crude, broad, triangular, stemless, white quartz arrow points than points of other shapes and materials; while in western Long Island the triangular form is in the minority. A similar state of affairs, exists in the shell-heaps of eastern Connecticut[1] the significance of which will be seen later. Another feature in which the Shinnecock differed from the tribes about New York City was in the use of the circular stone pendant, seldom seen in the latter district.

When the writer visited Shinnecock in 1902 he found the language dead, and was able to collect only the few words given below, although it was afterward learned that there were persons, living away from the settlement, who might have furnished at least a much larger vocabulary. The list is given for what it is worth, with a few suggestive comparisons, merely with the comment that the first two words were found also among the Poosepatuck mixed-bloods on Long Island.[2]

It will be noticed that there are many more correspondences between Shinnecock and Natick and Narragansett than between Shinnecock and Delaware, Abnaki or Sauk, and that Narragansett seems nearest of all on account of the remarkably close resemblance of some of the rarer words. It is also interesting to note that good cognates in Algonkian dialects were easily found for all the Shinnecock words collected except the greeting "hah'cami."

The writer makes no claim to a knowledge of Algonkian languages and has probably overlooked important evidence, but it seems safe to state, on the basis of this brief vocabulary alone, that the Shinnecock language was more nearly related to the Southern New England group of Algonkian dialects than it was to the Lenapé (Delaware) group or to the Abnaki group, and this same conclusion has been reached independently by Speck[1] and by Tooker.[2]

Archæologically, we have the evidence of the wide triangular white quartz arrow points, before mentioned, as a favorite form, the pottery, the decoration on the earthern pipes, and the antler fish hooks, connecting the Shinnecock material culture with that of southern New England, particularily eastern Connecticut, but further investigation is needed in both regions before we can make full comparisons and be certain of Shinnecock relationship in this respect. Such comparisons would be particularly interesting in view of the fact that the Shinnecock kept their ancient culture, if not their blood, pure to the last, unmodified by the Iroquois influence that had made itself so strongly felt about the mouth of the Hudson and even in many parts of New England shortly before the arrival of the whites.

---

[1]In the collection of Mr. Norris L. Bull of Hartford, Connecticut, may be seen rude triangular quartz arrow points, antler fish hooks, forms and decorations of pottery, and decorations on earthern pipes, practically identical in detail with those found at Shinnecock Hills. These were discovered in a shell-heap near the mouth of the Niantic River. Specimens from shell-heaps further west, near Milford, for example, do not show this close resemblance.

[2]The Natick and Narragansett words are from Trumbull, James Hammond, "Natick Dictionary" (*Bulletin 25, Bureau of American Ethnology*, Washington, 1903); the Delaware from Brinton, Daniel G. and Anthony, Albert S., "A Lenâpé-English Dictionary" (*Pennsylvania Students Series*, vol. 1, Historical Society of Pennsylvania, Philadelphia, 1888), plus one word, säpan, collected by myself; the Abnaki is from Elijah Tahomont, an Abnaki of St. Francis, Quebec; the Malecite is from Dr. Frank G. Speck; while the Sauk is from the late Dr. William Jones.

[1]Dr. Frank G. Speck wrote me in a personal letter that he believes that the Shinnecock belong linguistically to the Southern New England group, and expresses the same idea in a manuscript, *Native Tribes and Dialects of Connecticut* to be published by the Bureau of American Ethnology.

[2]The similarity of the eastern Long Island and southern New England dialects is brought out in Tooker, William Wallace, *John Eliot's First Indian Teacher and Interpreter, Cockenoe-de-Long Island*, New York, 1896).

Judging from the conditions noted at Sebonac, we might conclude that wherever the Shinnecock came from, they had not been located in eastern Long Island more than a few hundred years before the coming of the whites; but we cannot state this as a fact, for other sites may be found showing longer occupation. This is another question to be settled by further explorations, which might also reveal the identity of their predecessors, whose existence was suggested by the finding of a few archaic, apparently non-Shinnecock specimens below our village layer.

CACHE OF BLADES FROM LONG ISLAND

Foster H. Saville

It is well known to have been the custom of Indians to hide, or cache, in the ground or the snow, or beneath a cairn, for security until needed, stores of surplus provisions, as well as such implements and other articles as were not immediately required or were difficult to transport. Sometimes caches of implements were made evidently for religious reasons, if one may judge by the manner of their disposal and by the fact that often the objects are beautifully chipped and bear no indication of ever having been put to use.

Many of the buried stores of perishable materials, such as food, having been forgotten or for some other reason were never recovered by their owners, soon practically disappeared; but others, consisting of objects made of such almost indestructible materials as stone, bone, copper and shell, are occasionally unearthed in the old Indian country.

Within the limits of Long Island, New York, two long-forgotten caches of stone implements have been discovered. In the spring of 1863, William Brower, while plowing a field bordering the creek flowing to Rockaway Landing, near Rockville Center, discovered a cache of two copper axes and two of stone, surrounded by a hundred chipped blades of black chert set upright in a circle. By reason of the position of these objects, the cache was probably a ceremonial one, not intended to be recovered. Two examples from this cache are shown in fig. 17.

The second Long Island cache of stone implements was found by Mr. John Messenger at Indian Neck, Peconic, in July, 1924, and presented by him to the Museum, as mentioned in a brief note in *Indian Notes* for January, 1925. The position of the implements when uncovered was in no sense peculiar; indeed they were scattered throughout an area of six by eight feet. When buried they probably were close together, but had been disturbed by plowing.

This cache consisted of one hundred and fifty-one specimens of brown and black chert, of which one hundred and nine are leaf-shape blades with straight base, fairly uniform in shape but differing in size. The smallest is two and a half inches in length by two inches in maximum width, while the largest is seven and a quarter inches long by three and five-eighths inches wide. The remainder consists of forty-one flakes of varying shapes and sizes, from an inch and a half to four inches in length, and an inch to two and a half inches in width. The exceptional implement from the deposit is a small stemmed arrowpoint, seven-eighths by three-quarters of an inch. This specimen, together with others from the cache, are illustrated in fig. 18.

Fig. 17.—Blades from a cache at Rockaway Landing near Rockville Center, Long Island, in 1863

Fig. 18.—Blades and arrowpoint from a cache found at Peconic, Long Island, by Mr. John Messenger in 1924

Reprinted from Museum of the American Indian: Heye Foundation, INDIAN NOTES AND MONOGRAPHS, Vol. 3, No. 1, 1926.

A MATINECOC SITE ON LONG ISLAND

F. P. Orchard

For a short time during the summer of 1927 the writer conducted excavations at Beach Haven, Port Washington, on Manhasset bay, Long Island, at a point about five hundred yards west of Sands Point road, where once was situated a village of the Matinecoc, an Algonquian tribe. These people inhabited the northwest coast of the island from Newtown, Queens county, to Smithtown, Suffolk county, having villages at the sites of Flushing, Cow Harbor, Glen Cove, Cold Spring, and Huntington; but even before the advent of the whites they had become reduced, probably on account of the hostility of the Iroquois, to whom they paid tribute, so that by the year 1650 only fifty families remained.

Originally the Beach Haven site rose to eighty feet above the water and was heavily wooded, but the greater part has been cut away to provide sand and gravel for building operations, and lately the area has been leveled by the Beach Haven Development Company. Several springs afforded an ample supply of water to the Indian inhabitants, and the natural slope offered shelter from the north winds, while unlimited quantities of fish and mollusks, as well as an abundance of game, insured an excellent supply of animal food, as the presence of bones of bear, deer, and smaller mammals and birds, and of many shells, attests. Many of the larger animal bones had been cracked evidently for the purpose of extracting the marrow.

Scattered throughout the site were numerous pits, from 22 to 84 inches in diameter and from 16 to 73 inches in depth, all found within the dotted areas shown on the accompanying map (pl. II), which represent the superficial shell deposits. These pits were found where digging had been the easiest, the soil for the greater part being sandy. The purpose of the pits was to provide for the disposal of refuse, as well as facilities for steaming mollusks, hence some of the pits were filled with ordinary camp sweepings, while others were packed with the shells of oysters, hard and soft clams, scallops, and mussels, with occasionally a few conch-shells. Mammal, bird, and fish bones were also numerous in many of the refuse deposits, and the artifacts to be mentioned were also found in them.

Fig. 58.—Cooking-pot (restored) found in pit 3. Height, 7¾ in. (15/8600)

The writer wishes to acknowledge the courtesies extended by Messrs Harry and F. L. Goodwin, and by the Beach Haven Development Company. Through their friendly interest the Messrs Good-

Fig. 59.—Rim fragment of a jar with incised decoration. Length, 4½ in. (14/7851)

Reprinted from Museum of the American Indian: Heye Foundation, INDIAN NOTES AND MONOGRAPHS, Vol. 5, No. 3, 1928.

win made it possible for us to uncover many shell-pits, as well as the burials, by operating their steam-shovel at points where we were not immediately engaged in excavation.

Of the artifacts recovered, chipped implements are represented especially by stemmed or notched and triangular arrowpoints. The latter, by far

Fig. 60.—Pottery vessel of Iroquois type with incised decoration, from northern Pennsylvania (After W. H. Holmes)

the more abundant, are chiefly of quartzite, although some are of yellow jasper and a few of black flint. The stemmed points are mainly of quartzite and argillite.

Net-sinkers were fashioned from flattish oval pebbles that were roughly notched by chipping at opposite edges and deeply enough to insure proper fastening to the net.

Hammerstones vary from simple pebbles without intentional alteration to those purposely pitted on two faces as an aid in grasping. All are more or less worn by use.

Stone pestles were used, as shown by many fragments. Some of these implements appear to have been made from long slivers, pecked to remove the sharp edges, and rubbed down with the aid of sand and water on the even surface of another stone.

A mortar with a depression pecked in one side was found, the reverse side showing signs of use in grinding rather than in pounding.

The pottery vessels of the Beach Haven site were of the characteristically Algonquian type, as well as of that class exhibiting strong Iroquois influence. A number of the fragments recovered are similar in pattern to one illustrated by Skinner,[1] having incised decoration from the rim to the slightly bulging body below the neck. An incised vessel found in pit 3 is illustrated in fig. 58 and will be referred to later. The sides and bottom of the vessels were often embellished by means of a cord-wrapped paddle, giving them the appearance of having been pressed with a woven fabric while the clay was moist. One pottery fragment bears

Fig. 61.—Pottery smoking-pipe. Length, 4 in. (Property of Mr. F. L. Goodwin)

an incised decoration like that of a vessel found in an Iroquois grave in northern Pennsylvania;[2] both are rounded at the base and each has a slightly constricted neck (figs. 59, 60).

Among the objects of earthenware is a complete plain tubular pipe found with a burial uncovered by a steam shovel, the bowl slightly expanded and with a fragment of what had been a bone stem (fig. 61). From the neighboring Cow Harbor site, Mr. Harrington many years ago found a pottery effigy of a human head that had formed part of a pipe bowl.[3]

Bone implements were few. Two awls, one embellished with an incised decoration at the thick end, the other plain, were found in pit 18. Another bone implement, with a rather blunt point, may have been employed in producing the incised decoration on pottery, as it was found in refuse that had filled a pit where clay had been removed.

A cup consisting of the bony carapace of a box-turtle, scraped and cleaned inside, the ribs having been cut away from the covering to fit it for use, was among the utilitarian objects recovered from pit 18.

The following pits contained objects of greater or lesser interest:

In pit 1 was a fireplace composed of three water-worn stones forming a triangle covering an area of 22 inches by 20 inches, and having a depth of 16 inches. Between the stones was a deposit of charcoal and small fragments of oyster-shell. One straight piece of charcoal, about an inch in diameter and eleven inches in length, appeared as if it might have been a handle of an implement, such as a stone ax or possibly a celt.

Pit 2 contained a deposit of broken shells about 24 inches in diameter and 10 inches in depth. The shells were quite compact and lay on sand, four inches deep, which had been subjected to sufficient heat to impart a brick-red color. Below the sand layer was a solid mass of ash, charcoal, and the calcined bones of a child, the surrounding earth being discolored by fire for a depth of 6 inches. Beneath the human remains was a bowl-shape deposit of clam-shells 5 inches in depth.

Pit 3, readily located by the discoloration of the black surface soil, which was composed mostly of charcoal and burned sand, covered a space 34 inches in length by 25 inches in width. The deposit, 23 inches in depth, contained six fire-stones forming a hearth two or three inches from the bottom of the pit. Several small potsherds and cracked animal bones were scattered throughout. At the northwest side of the fireplace lay a cooking-pot in two large fragments, and many small sherds were uncovered nearby (fig. 62). Beneath the larger sherds were fragments of cracked animal bones and several pieces of sturgeon plate. These remains were mixed with what may have been fat which presumably the vessel had contained. The vessel represented by the larger sherds is shown, restored, in fig. 58. Its ornamentation consists of rude horizontal incised lines from the rim to almost half-way down the body.

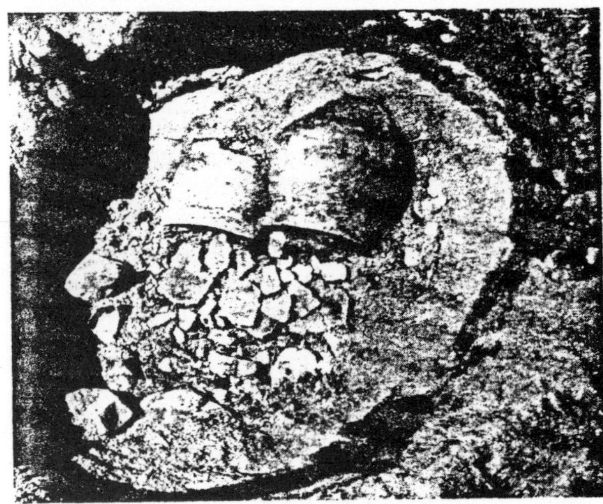

Fig. 62.—Cooking-pot at the edge of a fireplace in pit 3. (15/8600)

In pit 4, partly removed by a steam-shovel, was the skeleton of an adult, the skull directed southwestward, the body flexed. The grave soil was much disturbed and mixed with ashes, oyster-shells, and animal bones. The outline of the grave was 58 inches by 38 inches, and was 36 inches in depth. About 21 inches below the skull was an oval of oyster-shells set on edge about five inches apart, and twelve inches lower was the complete skeleton of a dog, 26 inches from head to tail, the body apparently having been carefully buried (fig. 63).

The remains of a double burial in pit 5, about 12 feet west of the burial described, consisted of the bones of an adult and an adolescent. The grave outline measured 70 inches by 16 inches, and was 44 inches in depth. The skull of the adult was directed southwestward; the body lay on its left side, with legs greatly flexed. The bones of the younger person, badly decayed, lay beneath those of the older, its skull directed northwestward (fig. 64). Thirty inches beneath these skeletons were the remains of a dog, represented by little more than stains, excepting the skull and the leg bones.

Fig. 63.—Skeleton of a dog in pit 4

Fig. 64.—Grave of an adult and an adolescent in pit 5

In pit 7, embedded in a large deposit of shells of

oysters, hard-clams, mussels, and scallops, were the remains of another human skeleton. The foot bones were eighteen inches beneath the surface, and the legs and pelvis seven inches deeper. Below these was an indurated deposit of clam-shells, 42 inches in diameter and 50 inches in depth. Several potsherds, a bone awl, and a black flint drill-point were found nearby.

Pit 8 contained a disturbed human burial consisting only of the skull, pelvis, femora, several fragments of ribs, and five vertebræ. A few potsherds and a portion of the stem of a pottery pipe were found in the grave. The grave outline was 39 inches long by 30 inches wide and 38 inches deep.

Pits 9, 10, and 11 contained shells, much charcoal, and mammal and fish bones. They ranged in size from 48 inches in diameter and 42 inches in depth, to 75 inches in diameter and 68 inches in depth.

The contents of pit 12 consisted of kitchen refuse, including shells, with which were a pitted hammerstone and a rectangular rubbing stone, one face of the latter having been worn flat and almost polished. This deposit was 57 inches in diameter and 48 inches in depth.

Pit 13 contained a deposit of hard-clam shells, with about three inches of ashes at the bottom. The sides of the pit had been subjected to sufficient heat to discolor the earth to an average depth of four inches. This pit had evidently been dug primarily for the purpose of steaming clams, the embers having first been removed and the clams placed between layers of seaweed, the whole then being sealed with earth until the contents were cooked. This deposit filled a depression 69 inches in diameter by 49 inches in depth.

Pits 14, 15, 16, and 17 were filled with shells, the holes evidently having been dug for the sole purpose of disposing of them. The pits were each about 48 inches in diameter and 36 inches in depth.

Pit 18, also designed to contain refuse, was 48 inches in diameter by 35 inches deep. In clearing this pit the turtle-shell cup, four net-sinkers, the two bone awls described, a fragment of a stone pestle, several potsherds, fish and animal bones, and charcoal were found.

Pit 20 was filled with many large oyster-shells, the largest being 11¾ inches long and 5½ inches wide. The cavity measured 30 inches long, 27 inches wide, and 33 inches deep.

Pit 22 likewise contained a refuse deposit, in this case consisting of many varieties of shellfish, animal bones, a few pot-rim sherds, a fragment of a steatite pipe bowl, a slim quartzite arrowpoint, and a bone awl. The pit measured 74 inches long, 59 inches wide, and 68 inches deep.

Pits 19, 21, 24, and 25 were packed with shells and other refuse and ranged in size from 44 inches in diameter by 32 inches in depth, to 87 inches long, 62 inches wide, and 73 inches deep. They were all rectangular, with rounded bottoms. Many conch-shells, black-fish jaw-bones, and mammal bones were found.

Pit 23 contained a fireplace, 11 inches in depth, covering a space of 29 inches in length and 24 inches in width. Three large irregular field stones formed the hearth, and at its edges were much charcoal and ash, and several potsherds.

[1] Skinner, A., Archeology of the New York Coastal Algonkin, *Anthr. Papers Amer. Mus. Nat. Hist.*, vol. III, p. 223, fig. 35, *b*, New York, 1909.

[2] See Holmes, W. H., in *Twentieth Ann. Rep. Bur. Amer. Ethnol.*, pl. CXIV, *b*, Washington, 1903.

[3] See Skinner, op. cit., p. 222, New York, 1909.

ARCHEOLOGICAL EXPLORATION OF FISHERS ISLAND, NEW YORK

BY

HENRY L. FERGUSON

INTRODUCTION

From early Colonial days until 1895, no record is known of the finding of any Indian artifacts on Fishers Island. About that year a grooved axe, now in the author's collection, was turned up by a plow in one of the fields of Durfee Meadow at the west end of the Island. Some few years later, Mr. W. W. Holmes, of Waterbury, Connecticut, who was interested in archeology, found some artifacts which are now in the museum of the Mattatuck Historical Society in his home city. It was not until 1912, when the author moved to the Island, that the systematic collection of Indian artifacts was commenced. From that year until 1924 farming was carried on throughout the Island, and the specimens found represented purely surface material. After that date the farm lands were uncultivated, and the surface finds gradually ceased. For several years little work was done, but in 1929 some excavating was accomplished in one shell heap, and the following year, really serious work was started. Possibly the results to date lack full scientific value, as proper records have not been kept; but the work so far completed has at least been done carefully, and it is felt that what ground has been gone over, has been thoroughly searched. It is hoped that the following report will add something of value to present information concerning the culture of the Indians occupying Fishers Island in pre-Colonial times. Later reports, it is hoped, will present a more complete record of future work. The author desires here to express his sincere thanks to Mr. Blair S. Williams, to Mr. William Shirley Fulton, and to Mr. Harold J. Baker who have all so enthusiastically assisted in the collecting, and who have permitted him to photograph many specimens from their personal collections, some of which are reproduced in the plates illustrating this paper. Also, he is deeply indebted to Mr. George G. Goodwin, Assistant Curator of the Department of Mammalogy, American Museum of Natural History, New York City, for his identification of the animal and other bones found during the research.

HISTORICAL NOTE

Fishers Island, called by the Indians *Munnawtawkit*, lies at the eastern end of Long Island Sound, its nearest point to the mainland being only two miles from the Connecticut shore. Prior to the coming of the white colonists, the Island was heavily wooded, and deer and game birds abounded on it. It was not until 1815 that the appearance changed, and then a great gale laid waste the Island and left it nearly denuded of trees. Good harbors afforded safe camp sites, and springs and fresh water lakes were near at hand. Clams and other shell fish were found in never failing supply, and, with game on land and fish plentiful in the waters about the Island, the Indians who lived there, or who visited it, had no difficulty in securing necessary food.

The earliest records state that the Connecticut coast from Niantic to what is now the Rhode Island state line was originally controlled by the Niantic. Some time previous to the coming of the whites, the Pequot, who were part of the Mohegan living on the Thames River, inland from New London, broke away from their main tribal body and forced their way southward to the coast, dividing the Niantic. The Narragansett occupied land east of the Rhode Island boundary, only distant from Fishers Island about four miles. Just which tribe of Indians came and hunted and fished and lived on the Island will probably never be known. Certainly the Niantic, Pequot, Mohegan, and Narragansett all lived near enough to make the journey in safety, but at the time the colonists reached Connecticut, the Pequot were in power.

For two years previous to 1637, John Winthrop, Jr., and Lion Gardiner had endeavored to found a settlement at Saybrook at the mouth of the Connecticut River. Continual trouble with the Indians resulted in May, 1637, in sending an expedition of ninety men led by Captain John Mason and Captain Underhill against the Pequot. Proceeding to Mystic, the whites surprised and killed six or seven hundred Indians, completely breaking the power of the Pequot. The survivors escaped and scattered.

Reprinted from Museum of the American Indian: Heye Foundation, INDIAN NOTES AND MONOGRPAHS, Vol. 11, No. 1, 1935.

One band was rounded up at Fairfield and butchered, and from that time the settlers were safe to take up land and begin colonizing the State.

Three years after the Pequot Massacre, John Winthrop, Jr., applied to the General Court of Massachusetts for a grant to Fishers Island, and the following year he applied to Connecticut for a similar one. In 1644 he purchased the title to the Island from the Indians, and twenty years later received a grant for it from the Duke of York. He was well protected in his ownership. In the year of the purchase from the Indians (1644), Winthrop moved to the Island, and his was the only white man's house between the Connecticut River and the Providence Plantations far to the east.

The only trouble Winthrop experienced with the Indians, the first winter, was when Nowequa, a brother of Uncas, came from the mainland and destroyed a canoe. For this act he was forced to pay one hundred fathoms of wampum. From old records, chiefly letters of the Winthrop family, we learn that Indians were later used on the Island as laborers for a number of years. Foundations of several small houses, of which there is no record, have been found on the Island and may mark the homes of these Indian workmen.

ARCHEOLOGICAL EXPLORATION OF FISHERS ISLAND, NEW YORK

HENRY L. FERGUSON

ARTIFACTS found on Fishers Island since 1912 have been grouped as surface finds; finds in connection with stray burials; and finds in connection with shell heaps. While these specimens are more fully described later in this paper, and classified as to material composition and use, it is considered advisable here to list the various locations with such collated information as may seem of interest and importance.

Surface Finds

The following different locations contained sufficient relics to designate them as probable camp sites. Each had water easily accessible. In addition to these areas, odd artifacts of stone and pottery have been found in various places removed from obvious or probable camp sites.

Hay Harbor; grooved axe.
Hawks Nest Point—West Harbor; fragments of stone bowl, stone points and chips.
Peninsula—West Harbor; stone points, limonite pendant, and other specimens; complete list of finds not available.
Sand Bank—West Harbor; fragments of badly decomposed skeleton, potsherds, crude stone points.
Wilderness Farm; stone points, potsherds.
Hill Field—Wilderness Swamp; stone points, potsherds.
Brick Yard, West—West Harbor; celt, stone points, potsherds.
Brick Yard, East—near Barlow Pond; stone points over a large area; fragments of stone bowls.
Beach—Middle Farm—North Shore; grooved axe, hammer stone, stone scrapers, points, and one net sinker.
Pond—Middle Farm; stone pestle.
Durfee Meadow; pottery bird's head; grooved axe.
Chocomount Cove; potsherds, object of metal. The land here has not been plowed.
Coast Guard Field; fragments of stone bowls, broken stone gorget, stone hoes, points and chips, potsherds, pottery pipe stem, pottery gaming disc.
Winthrop Fields; celt, hammer stones, stone mortar, points, gouge, and a limonite paint stone.
Reservation Field; broken banner stone, fragment of stone gorget, stone points, potsherds, pottery pipe stem.
Grass Pond; stone chips, potsherds.
Ponds; several good points have been picked up along the edges of the Island's many ponds when the water levels have fallen. In all probability these were used or lost while fishing or hunting.

Stray Burials

have been located from time to time, by accident, in widely scattered locations on the Island. These points are designated by numbered crosses on the map. That burial accompaniments were found with only two of these burials, probably points more to carelessness or disinterest among those excavating rather then to an actual lack of such artifacts. In no instance was any record made of the position of the skeletons nor of the depth at which they were found. From accounts, all were in shallow graves.

BURIAL NO. 1. This skeleton was found when widening the road near Fort Wright gate. With it were found a fragment of a brass object, a limonite paint cup, and a lead bullet. No record of the position of the skeleton was made by the workmen, who merely gathered up what they happened to see.

BURIALS NOS. 2 & 3. About 1895 two skeletons were dug up by C. W. Hedge while putting in a pipe line. No records were made.

BURIAL NO. 4. While excavating for the cellar of the Walker house, a laborer drove a pick into a skull. This was saved with some of the other bones. A rumor, probably with some truth in it, says that a bead necklace was found. If so, it has not as yet been traced.

BURIAL NO. 5. In 1926, while excavating for the Fishers Island Club, laborers dug into a stone lined grave, and destroyed it before notes or pictures could be made. No artifacts were found.

BURIAL NO. 6. A skeleton, without discernible accompaniments, was found and reburied while grading was in progress at the Reed property on Hungry Point.

BURIAL NO. 7. While constructing the seventh green on the golf course in 1926, a scraper turned up a skeleton in white sand. The skull was lost, having been dumped in the fill before the bones were noticed. With this burial a perforated black stone pebble ornament (pl. IX, *a*) was found.

BURIAL NO. 8. This skeleton, of an adult, was found near the ocean on the south side of the Wilderness Swamp while putting in a pipe line. No artifacts accompanied it.

BURIAL NO. 9. A child's skeleton was uncovered

on the high land east of East Harbor while widening the road. No artifacts were found.

Shell Heap Burials

In two of the shell heaps so far worked, Hedge and Peninsula, complete or partial skeletons were found.

HEDGE. The first burial encountered was exhumed from shells at a depth of 18 in. It proved to be the skeleton of a child of about ten years of age, and was a reburial. The skull was badly crushed, and was placed where the pelvis should have been, facing east. The pelvic, arm, and finger bones were placed where the skull should have been. The leg bones were missing. A bone bodkin was found with this burial.

The next burial was found 2 ft. beneath the surface, and was also a reburial. The bones lay in a fire pit covered by 1½ ft. of shells and 6 in. of topsoil, and reposing upon 1 ft. of ashes and shells. The skeleton was in a flexed position. The skull, though badly crushed, was in proper relation to the spine, facing southeast. The arm bones were laid across the pelvis, the leg bones being missing. In the stomach position were found the skeletons of two fish and several clam shells. These latter were in pairs showing that the bivalves were whole when placed in position. The scales and bones of the fish were well preserved. Nothing else was found directly with this burial, but within a radius of 2 ft., and within the same pit, bone and stone implements and some potsherds were found.

About 1 ft. nearer the surface and the same distance to the southeast of this burial, another skull was found with parts of the jaw bones missing. No other bones were located.

Four feet southeast of the second burial, and about 3 ft. beneath the surface, on the edge of a fire pit, were found pieces of another skull, the whole of which when restored would measure approximately 5 in. in diameter. In this instance, too, no other bones were found.

Four feet west of the third burial, another reburial was encountered. This skeleton was badly dismembered and broken. The arm and leg bones were missing.

PENINSULA. In the first area uncovered, a burial in perfect condition was exhumed. The skeleton was that of an aged person buried in a flexed position nearly east and west with the skull facing south. No accompaniments of any description were found in connection with the bones.

Shell Heaps

The shell heaps on the Island are not large in area, and, except in two instances, lie under about 7 in. of top soil and have an 8 in. average depth of shells, mostly of long clams, badly broken. In these two deposits, the shell layers vary from a few inches to three feet in thickness. In the shell heaps so far excavated, and in the top soil overlying them, not a single article of European manufacture has been found, except where the owner of an adjoining house had buried refuse, though the regular layers of shells and the pits have yielded a variety of Indian artifacts. The locations of the shell heaps are designated on the map by circled capitals.

HAWKS NEST POINT (A). This midden lies at the southern part of a hill near the site of the original camp. It measures 300 ft. long by 70 ft. wide, and runs from high water-mark inland. The surface area was formerly plowed, and the topsoil is, therefore, mixed with small pieces of shell. Excavation was commenced near the road and carried westward, revealing one pit after another, often only a foot apart, and varying in depth from 3 ft. to 4½ ft. Some pits were full of long clam shells, some, of round clams, and two contained only scallop shells. In most of the pits, some oyster and mussel shells were found scattered throughout. No burial was encountered here, but it is possible that graves may be encountered higher up on the hillside. This midden has yielded so far half of a broken boat-stone, a slate ornament, a celt, hammer stones, sinkers, stone scrapers, bone awls, points, and many potsherds. Fish and deer bones were found throughout, and a piece of moose antler and fish hooks were recovered.

HEDGE SHELL HEAP (C). A fine spring, which is now filled up, furnished water for the camp site which was probably situated on the hill-top north of the deposit. The shell heap lies in a hollow of the hills, and this whole site affords one of the best sheltered places on the Island for camping. The surface soil has been plowed, and as the area has been used for many years as a chicken yard, broken shells and surface refuse abound. Excavations here have been carried on in three separate sections. The entire area opened in Section A approximates 28 ft. square, and 6 in. below the surface, the first layer of shells averaged 8 in. in thickness. From appearances, the deepest parts of this midden, except for three or four pits, appear to follow the contour of the ground, which slopes gradually and is clearly not dug. In the autumn of 1933, at a depth of 5 ft., beneath two distinct deposits of shells, and in 5 in. of yellow sand, a skeleton of a seal, minus the skull, was uncovered. A bone harpoon point (pl. XIII, *n.*) was found among the bones. Near it was found the boat-stone shown in pl. IX, *b*. This section of Hedge has yielded potsherds, occasional arrow points and hammer stones, and bone needles and awls.

Section B, an area about 12 ft. by 44 ft., lies 35 ft. northeast of A, at the base of the hill slope, and a road has covered this deposit for years. As new cement pavement was to be laid, digging in this area was pushed with all haste. Shells were encountered at a depth of 4 in. and continued downward for about 3 ft. Several pits were found, all about 3 ft. in diameter and 4 ft. in depth. In one section where mussel shells abounded, about three-quarters of a jar, shown restored in the frontispiece, was found. Potsherds, pieces of stone pipe bowls, a gaming stone, bone awls and pins, and several stone mortars were found among the shell layers. Some of the pottery pieces had disintegrated and could not be saved.

Section C was opened due northward from the center of B for 20 ft. at a width of 10 ft. For half the distance the average depth of the topsoil was 8 in. Beneath this, the shell stratum measured about 16 in. with 4 in. of underlying ash. Early in the digging, a pit measuring $4\frac{1}{2}$ ft. by 3 ft. deep was located, though nothing was found in it save a few potsherds and some animal bones. The earlier laying of a pipe line had ruined much of the structure and contents of this pit. Between two boulders on the western boundary of the excavation, another fire pit was located and opened. This section has yielded a bone bead, bone awls, a slender pestle-like stone, a broken, badly decomposed, ornamented pot and a clam shell dipper (pl. XI, *g*.).

BRICK YARD—EAST (G). This shell heap lies in a hollow about 75 yds. from Barlow Pond, and the entire area from about 200 yds. south and west has furnished surface finds. This is a small deposit, measuring only 100 ft. by 25 ft. Two pits and no burials were found in it. About 8 in. of top soil covers the layer of shells which varies from 1 in. to 4 in. in depth. Only a portion of this heap has been searched and has yielded a shell spoon, a broken bone fish hook, bone awls, hammer stones, arrow points, and a crude axe. Broken pottery, in useless fragments, and the usual quantities of animal bones were found throughout.

PENINSULA (D). About 5 in. of top soil covers this deposit, and a spring is located at its southern edge where the marsh commences. It was in the first section dug, an area about 8 ft. by 5 ft., that the undisturbed burial was found. Twenty feet east of this excavation another pit was started before work was discontinued for the winter. The shell heap measures 30 ft. by 60 ft., and has an average depth of 2 ft. from the surface. Arrow points, a graphite paint stone, and potsherds were found.

BAY VIEW (B). This deposit lies at the water's edge, and has an area of 150 ft. by 90 ft., and only one pit has been excavated. The topsoil was mixed with shells to a depth of 12 in. beneath which an 8 in. layer of shells was found. Beneath this was a stratum of yellow dirt about 6 in. thick, and below, shells continued downward for more than 2 ft. In fact, the layer was not dug through. The shells of the lower deposit were nearly all those of long clams, their interiors browned as from roasting. This is the only shell heap yet found with a thick stratum of these unbroken and scorched shells. Stone chips and potsherds were encountered throughout.

Five additional shell heaps have been located, but remain as yet untouched. They are Holmes (E), Brick Yard—West (F), North Hill (H), Mansion House Field (I), and Barlow (J).

Description of Artifacts

ARTICLES OF STONE

Axes. There have not been many axes found, and those that have been recovered are all of the completely grooved type. Representative ones are shown on pl. V. The best one (*c*) is finely finished and is $9\frac{3}{4}$ in. long, with a circumference of $10\frac{1}{2}$ in. about the ridge nearest the cutting edge. This was found near the entrance of Hay Harbor. It weighs $6\frac{1}{4}$ lbs. and is made of a claystone porphyry. Two comparable axes have also been found. These are not available for measurement or description. One crude grooved axe (*a*) was found on the beach at Middle Farm, on the north shore of the Island. Those shown as *b* and *d* are of different form.

Banner Stone. The half of a black basalt banner stone of the bipointed type, with large transverse perforation (pl. IX, *i*) similar to the type found in the Ohio valley, came from Reservation Field.

Boat Stones. In one of the pits opened in Hawks Nest Shell Heap a fragment of a broken slate boat stone was recovered (pl. IX, *j*). This shows no evidences of perforation. Another fragment (*b*) of a steatite one was found at Hedge Shell Heap. It has two perforations, one at the end and one on top; next to the latter, on the broken edge, are traces of a third one, and on the concave side the start of still another is in evidence. On the top it has been scored with several incised lines.

Celts. One good celt (pl. VI, *d*) was found on the surface at Brick Yard—West. This measures $3\frac{5}{8}$ in. in length and has a circumference of $3\frac{5}{8}$ in. A small but perfect implement (*e*) of this type was found on the surface of the high ground to the south of the present eighth green of the golf course—old Winthrop Fields. Both of these specimens are of the petaloid type. The cutting edges of two broken celts were excavated near the second burial exhumed from Hedge Shell Heap. Another celt, a stone with natural depressions on the sides and with a well worked edge, was recovered from Hawks Nest Shell Heap.

Chipped Points. Plates I, II, and III depict types of arrow and spear points, knife blades, scrapers and perforators, of shapes and materials similarly used on the adjacent mainland. Many were recovered as surface finds from Hawks Nest Point; Peninsula—West Harbor; Sand Bank—West Harbor; Wilderness Farm—Hill Field; Brick Yard—West; over a large area at Brick Yard—East; on the beach at Middle Farm (yielded over two hundred); Coast Guard Field; Winthrop Fields; Reservation Field; and from the banks of several ponds at low-water level.

Close to the second burial uncovered in Hedge Shell Heap, a small point was found with the broken celts and bone awls. These were about 2 ft. under the surface among the shells. Other points were also found during the digging at Hedge. A few points were recovered from shell layers at Brick Yard—East and one point from Peninsula Shell Heap.

Chips have been found in quantities on the surface at Hawks Nest Point, Coast Guard Field, on elevations near Grass Pond, east of the golf course, and in the shell deposit at Bay View.

Dishes. Fragments of a soapstone dish were found with many arrow points and chips on the surface of the high ground above the shell deposit at Hawks Nest Point. Other fragments of similar steatite bowls have been found on the East Brick Yard Field and on the Coast Guard Field.

Gaming Stone. One flat, circular stone (pl. VI, *b*), of the type sometimes referred to as "chunke stones," was obtained at Hedge Shell Heap. This has been fashioned from an irregular slab of stone and shows no evidences of finishing on its flat surfaces.

Gorgets. Only three fragments of stone gorgets have been found. One of sandstone (pl. IX, *d*) shows, besides part of a perforation, two incised lines. This specimen comes from the surface of Coast Guard Field. Another one (*f*) of slate, also showing a perforation, was picked up on Reservation Field. The third fragment (*h*) is well finished and of a hard stone and was found in Hedge Shell Heap.

Gouge. Only one gouge has been found, and this a small one (pl. VI, *a*). The hollowing is but slight and starts about half-way down the blade. The cutting edge is sharp and shows considerable use. It is a crudely finished specimen, the pecking marks showing on the back of it. An unusual feature is that secondary chipping shows along one edge. It was found close to the eighth golf green near Winthrop House.

Grinding Stones. A few of this type of artifact were recovered, by far the most interesting being the one shown on pl. VII, *b*. Unfortunately, this specimen has been broken and part is missing. It is grooved on both sides, the depression shown being $2\frac{1}{8}$ in. wide and $\frac{7}{16}$ in. deep, while the one on the opposite side is $1\frac{3}{8}$ in. wide and $\frac{1}{8}$ in. deep. It was in all probability used in finishing pestles.

Another unusual grinding stone is depicted on pl. VI, *g*. It shows much use all over, and two surfaces (on the left) are so worn that they almost form a cutting edge where they meet.

Hammer Stones. A single hammer stone was found with other stone implements on the beach at Middle Farm. Several more have been recovered as surface finds on Winthrop Fields during construction work on the golf course. A variety of hammer stones were found scattered through all the sites in Hawks Nest, Hedge, and Brick Yard—East Shell Heaps.

Hoes. The only hoes as yet collected are four in number, three of which are shown in pl. IV. Two, (*a.* and *c.*) were surface finds in a section of Coast Guard Field, situated at the narrow neck of the island, near its eastern point. The largest one (*a*) $10\frac{1}{2}$ in. long, shows no evidence of having been used, while the other two do so to a slight extent; (*c*) is of the wide-blade, narrow-top type, the most convenient for hafting. The hoe not shown is also of this type. A great part of their surfaces have disintegrated, probably due to sand-blasting. That illustrated in pl. IV, *b* was found in Section B of Hedge Shell Heap.

Mortars. A small, flat mortar was found on the surface with other stone artifacts near the present eighth golf green, originally Winthrop Fields. Another has a depression on both sides. That shown on pl. VIII is $\frac{7}{8}$ in. deep, and the other $\frac{1}{2}$ in. This and several crude mortars have been recovered from Hedge Shell Heap.

Paint Cup. A limonite paint cup (pl. VI, *c*) was found with Stray Burial No. 1 near the gate to Fort Wright. The cup rested on a fragmentary brass ornament. The edge of the concretion has been ground smooth, as has also a projection on its base.

Paint Stones. Paint stones of both limonite (pl. IX, *e*) and graphite (*c*), showing much usage on their surfaces, have been frequently met with.

Pendants. An irregular, flat, black slate pendant (pl. IX, *g*), with a biconical perforation and the beginning of another adjacent to it, came from the shell heap at Hawks Nest Point.

Another pendant of a small natural pebble (pl. IX, *a*), also with a biconical drilling, was an accompaniment of Stray Burial No. 7.

A triangular shape limonite pendant was a surface find southeast of the peninsula in West Harbor. It measures $\frac{3}{4}$ in. wide at the perforated end, and is 1 in. long, with a thickness varying from $\frac{1}{32}$ in. to $\frac{1}{16}$ in. The perforation is $\frac{1}{16}$ in. in diameter and is of the biconical type. One surface is quite smooth, the other shows where it was split from a larger piece and then worked down by grinding. The edges have been worked down to shape.

Pestles. An artifact that might be classed as a pestle is a slender stone rod, $10\frac{1}{8}$ in. in length and having a circumference of $8\frac{7}{16}$ in. (pl. VII, *a*). This was recovered during low water on the edge of Middle Farm Pond. Both ends show much use, but the sides have not been worked. Several other broken pestles have been found in shell heaps or elsewhere.

Pipes. A fragment of soapstone pipe bowl, with cross-hatched decoration, was found in Hawks Nest Point Shell Heap. Parts of two other pipe bowls have also been uncovered in Hedge Shell Heap.

Scrapers. Small scrapers are shown on pl. I, *a*, *b*, and a large one, probably used in skin dressing, is pictured on pl. III, *a*. The objects *b* and *c* on the same plate might have also seen use as scrapers, but more probably they are unfinished blades. Drill points are depicted on pl. II, *a*, *b*, and the larger type of perforator on pl. II, *c* and pl. III, *d*.

Sinkers. Several natural stones grooved for use as net or fish-line sinkers (pl. VI, *h*, *i*) were recovered from the various shell heaps. These vary in size from $2\frac{3}{8}$ in. in diameter to $1\frac{1}{16}$ in. and are the type common to the New England shore districts. One notched net sinker (pl. VII, *c*) and another of similar type have been found.

Smoothing Stone. The only one recovered is illustrated on pl. VI, *f*. All surfaces show wear, particularly the ends. This was found in the Hedge Shell Heap.

OBJECTS OF BONE

Awls. Many examples of so-called awls have been recovered from the shell heap excavations. These seem to fall into three classes: the flat, perforated type (pl. XII, *i, j, k, l, m, n, o, p, q*); the heavy type (pl. XIII, *d, e*); and the pick-like type (pl. XIII, *f, g, h*). These latter are made from cracked bone, the point having been sharpened and the sides smoothed by rubbing. They are too small and delicate to have been used for drilling and were, possibly, implements for picking out the flesh from shellfish.

The perforated type does not have the appearance of being strong enough for drilling in most instances. Of the nine found, only one could be used practically for this purpose; the others, too, appear to be better suited for picks or forks for eating purposes. The perforation was probably used for a thong, to enable it being attached to a belt or part of the clothing.

Three awls, in good condition, were found near the second burial discovered in the Hedge Shell Heap, about 2 ft. under the surface; and perforated and plain awls have been recovered from other sections of this area, a great number from Section B. Some awls were found in each pit in the Hawks Nest midden.

Seven awls, of fine workmanship and in excellent condition, were found in the shell layers at Brick Yard—East. Three were of the perforated type and the rest, ordinary sharpened bones.

Arrow Points. One arrow point, made from the toe bone of a deer (pl. XII, *d*) and one of antler (*c*), were recovered from Hawks Nest Shell Heap. Another arrow point, fashioned from a bird bone (*b*), is interesting on account of the well shaped barbs on its base.

Beads. A bone bead (pl. XIII, *k*) measuring $1\frac{5}{8}$ in. in length was found in Hawks Nest Shell Heap. Two others (*i, l*) were recovered from Section C in Hedge Shell Heap. In the same area, two bones showing marks of circular cutting were also found. These, probably, were discarded in the process of bead manufacture. Two beads (pl. XII, *e*), made from fish vertebrae, were recovered from Hawks Nest Shell Heap.

Bodkins. One bodkin of the usual type, made from the ulna of some member of the deer family, is shown on pl. XIII, *o*. The fragment of a flat bodkin was found in the Hedge Shell Heap.

Fish Hooks. Three bone fish hooks, two perfect, the other broken by the trowel (pl. XII, *f, g, h*) were found, the entire ones in the shell deposit at Hawks Nest Point. These are nearly identical in shape, and each has a groove in which the line could be fastened. The broken one was recovered from Hedge Shell Heap.

Fish-hook Barb. Only one bone barb (pl. XII, *a*), of the type attached to a piece of wood or bone, has been found. A small groove for lashing purposes may be seen on the lower end.

Harpoon Point. The harpoon point (pl. XIII, *n*), found at a depth of 5 ft. among the bones of the seal burial in Section A at Hedge Shell Heap, is the remnant of what, originally, was a longer point, as is shown by the re-cut base. It presents two barbs on one side. A fragment of another is shown, *m*.

Knife Handle. A well shaped and preserved tool handle of antler (pl. XIII, *j*), probably for a knife, was discovered at Hedge Shell Heap.

Pins. Three bone pins were found in Hedge Shell Heap. One, $5\frac{7}{16}$ in. in length, has an oblong head, on which a cross-hatched design is carved (pl. XIII, *c*). The second (*a*), $6\frac{1}{8}$ in. long, was made from a deer bone and is not ornamented. The third, (*b*), $6\frac{5}{16}$ in. in length, is without any head, well tapered to a sharp point, and has three grooves near its base.

Scraper. A bone skin scraper (fig. 1.), broken at both ends, was found in Hedge Shell Heap. This was made from the rib of a member of the deer family. One side was worked down to an edge about as sharp as a paper cutter, the other being left natural.

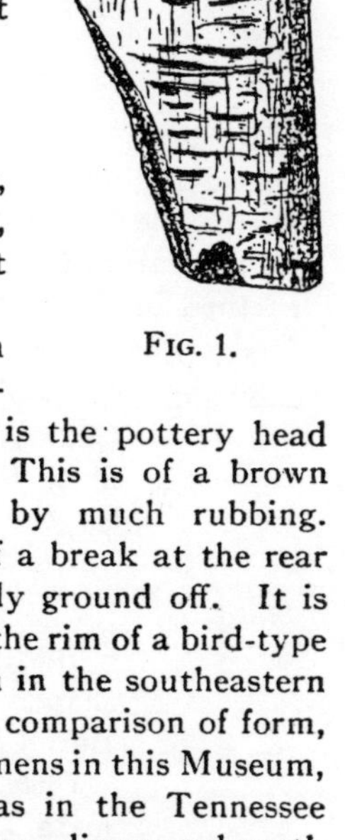

FIG. 1.

POTTERY

Bead. A fragment of a crude, barrel-shaped bead (pl. XI, *e*), $1\frac{3}{4}$ in. long, was obtained at Hedge Shell Heap.

Bird's Head. Probably in some ways the most interesting specimen yet met with is the pottery head of a crested bird (pl. XI, *a*). This is of a brown pottery and highly polished by much rubbing. Though still showing a trace of a break at the rear end, the base has been carefully ground off. It is without doubt the handle from the rim of a bird-type bowl, such as is often met with in the southeastern part of the United States. By comparison of form, clay, and finish with other specimens in this Museum, it is certain that its origin was in the Tennessee Valley. It is $1\frac{7}{16}$ in. high and was discovered north of the Durfee Meadow.

Gaming Disc. One pottery gaming disc (pl. XI, *d*), $1\frac{3}{16}$ in. in diameter, was found on the surface at the ancient camp site near the Coast Guard Station.

Jar. About three-quarters of an Iroquoian-type vessel (frontispiece) was recovered by Mr. Harold J. Baker from Section B of Hedge Shell Heap, and presented by him to the Museum of the American Indian, Heye Foundation (catalogue number 18/7403). This is a fine specimen, and is shown fully restored. It measures 12½ in. in height and is 11 in. wide at its greatest circumference. It has four points on the rim with nodes in front of them made by pinching the clay, when soft, between the thumb and forefinger. Below the rim is an incised decoration of lines and dots, and a band of the same at the lower part of the neck. The entire lower part of the jar has a paddled decoration of a twisted cord type, probably made by wrapping a string about a wooden paddle. It is of a uniform dark brown color and, from the evidence of carbon attached to it in places, was undoubtedly used as a cooking pot.

Pipe Stems. Pottery pipe stems, two in number, (pl. XI, *b*, *c*) were recovered from the Hedge Shell Heap. Two other pipe stems were found on the surface at the Coast Guard and Reservation Fields.

Potsherds (pl. X) have been found at many points on the surface of the Island and have been recovered from practically every shell heap. All of this pottery was so badly broken or scattered as to make any, save small restoration impossible. Most of the sherds found were well fired and are of good quality. Two colors predominate, a reddish brown and a slaty black, but some of dark brown are also met with. Some few pieces of vessel rims show typical Algonkian and Iroquois types of incised and punctate ornamentation, as may be seen by referring to the illustration. The Algonkian type predominates, by a rough estimate, two to one. Plate X, *a*, *b*, *d*, *j*, *k* and *l* show sherds of this culture, and *c*, *e*, *f*, *g*, *h*, and *i*, those from the Iroquois.

ARTICLES OF SHELL

Dipper. A large clam shell (pl. XI, *g*), worked considerably on its edge, was probably used as a food stirrer, the side of the pot wearing the edge away. It would naturally be used as a dipper. It was unearthed in the southeastern corner of Section C of Hedge Shell Heap.

Spcon. A spoon fashioned from a conch shell (pl. XI, *f*) was found at Brick Yard—East Shell Heap. This measures 3⅛ in. in length.

ARTICLES OF METAL

Bullet. A leaden bullet, much misshapen, was an accompaniment to Stray Burial No. 1.

Ornaments. A perforated object of metal (fig. 2), 4$\frac{5}{16}$ in. in length, was found on a sandy hillside near the Goodwin place on Chocomount Cove. It is made of brass, having been fashioned from some utensil of European manufacture, probably one of the brass kettles so commonly traded to the Indians in Colonial days. The perforation has not been drilled but has been punched out, thus casting doubt as to its aboriginal origin as an ornament.

The fragments of a badly decomposed brass ornament were found with Stray Burial No. 1, near the gate at Fort Wright. It lay among the bones on a fragment of bark, under a small stone paint cup. This object was also probably made from a brass utensil, as on one side of it there is still adhering to it some lead solder.

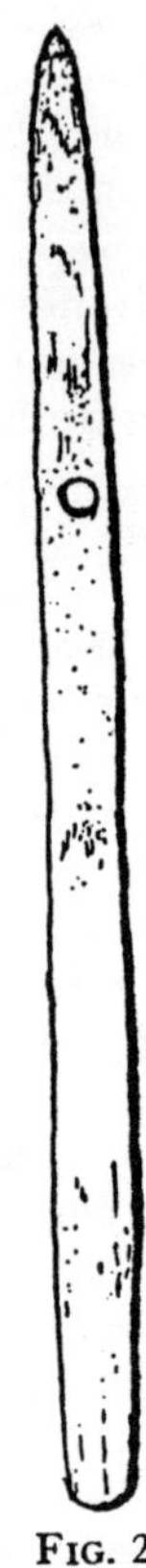

FIG. 2.

CONCLUSION

Until further research is accomplished, it is not advisable to express definite ideas as to results thus far. From the preliminary work done, there arise, however, several striking points, mostly of a negative character. One of the most interesting is the almost complete lack of relics showing contact with the white settler. With the exception of the two objects made from fragments of brass kettles (one of them from the surface, and, possibly, not used by the Indians), and the bullet, nothing has been recovered of Colonial origin.

It should be borne in mind that until 1644 the Indians inhabited the Island. In that year John Winthrop, Jr., completed his purchase and moved there. It is not conceivable that he would allow Indians in any number to live on the Island, because of fears for his family's safety in so isolated a location. The year 1644, therefore, was probably the last date that the camp sites could have been used as such by Indians. We know from records that in later years some Indians were employed as laborers. These most likely, lived in houses furnished by their employers.

It is doubtful if anything new of Indian workmanship has been discovered on Fishers Island, with the possible exception of the pestle grinder. Probably the three pins, the broken boat stone, the pottery bird's head, and the harpoon are of most interest. The varieties of awls show three types and most certainly were not all used for drilling.

A marked scarcity of ordinary shell beads and personal ornaments is noticeable, due undoubtedly to the fact that but a few scattered and unrecorded burials, and some reburials, have been unearthed. There is probably an Indian cemetery somewhere on the Island. When this is discovered, much more will be learned of its ancient inhabitants.

Many deer bones and the remains of other animals have been found. In the sea, fish and shell fish abounded, and birds were plentiful, so that the Indians did not have much labor in supplying their needs. Whether the Island was used only in the summer months, or whether the Indian inhabitants lived upon it all the year, cannot be definitely proven at the present time.

IDENTIFIED BONES

A large assortment of the bones and teeth that have been found while exploring the shell heaps, whether in the top soil or in the shell deposits themselves, was sent to the American Museum of Natural History for identification. The following list has been identified by Mr. G. G. Goodwin, Assistant Curator of Mammals.

ANIMALS

Beaver............... Castor canadensis (Kuhl)
Deer (Virginia)........ Odocoileus virginianus (Boddaert)
Dog (Domestic)....... Canis familiaris
Fox................. Vulpes fulva (Desmarest)
Mink................. Mustela vison mink (Peale and Beauvois)
Moose................ Alces americana (Clinton)
Muskrat.............. Ondatra zibethica (Linn.)
Otter................ Lutra canadensis (Schreber)
Ox (Domestic)......... Bos domestica
Pig (Domestic)......... Sus scrofa domestica
Porpoise.............. Sp. (?)
Seal (Harbor)......... Phoca vitulina concolor (De Kay)
Sheep (Domestic)...... Ovis domestica
Woodchuck........... Marmota monax (Linn.)

BIRDS

Duck (Golden eye)..... Clangula clangula (Linn.)
Duck (Scoter)......... Oidemia sp. (?)
Eagle (Golden)........ Aquila chrysaetos canadensis (Linn.)
Black Brant........... Branta nigricans (Lawr.)
Goose (Canada)....... Branta canadensis canadensis (Linn.)
Lesser Snow Goose..... Chen hyperborea hyperborea (Pallas)
Grouse (Ruffed)....... Bonasa umbellus umbellus (Linn.)
Gull.................. Lavus sp. (?)
Loon................. Gavia immer immer (Brunnich)
Merganser (American).. Mergus merganser americanus (Cassin)

FISH

Black Fish (Tautog).... Tautoga onitis (Linn.)
Dog Fish (Spined)..... Squalus acanthias (Linn.)
Shark (Sand).......... Carcharias littoralis (Mitchell)
Sheepshead............ Sparidae

REPTILES

Turtle (Painted)....... Chrysemis picta (Schneider)
Turtle (Snapping)...... Chelydra sepentina (Linn.)

FERGUSON—FISHERS ISLAND FRONTISPIECE

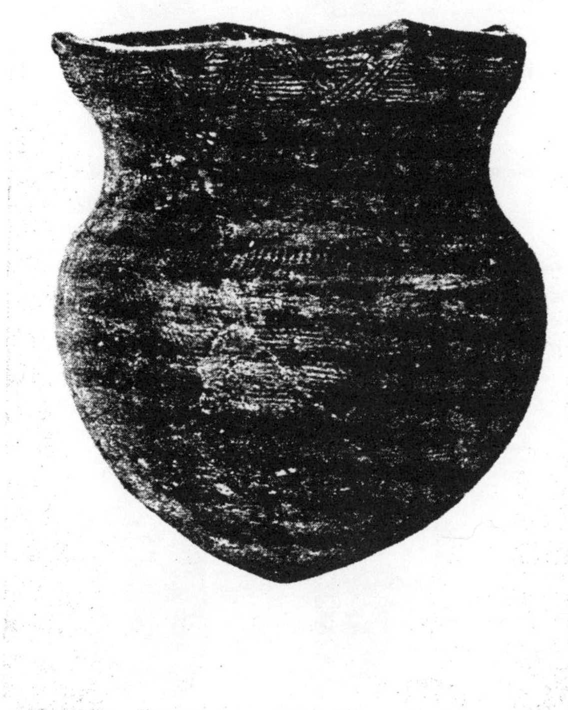

POTTERY VESSEL

In the Museum of the American Indian, Heye Foundation (Cat. No. 18/7403) Height, 12¼ inches

FERGUSON—FISHERS ISLAND PLATE I

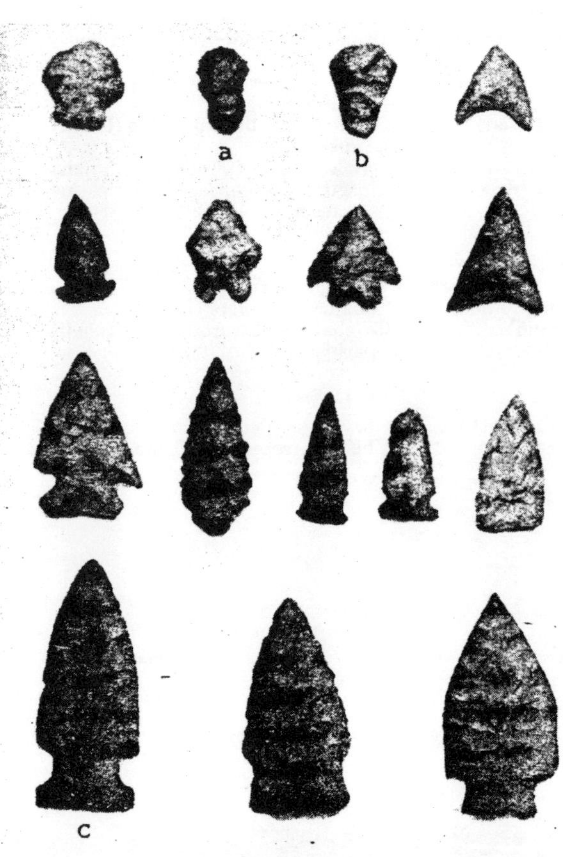

ARROW POINTS, SCRAPERS, AND SPEAR POINTS, OF STONE

Length of *c*, 3 $\frac{1}{16}$ inches

FERGUSON—FISHERS ISLAND PLATE II

ARROW POINTS, PERFORATORS AND KNIFE BLADES OF STONE

Length of *d*, 3$\frac{1}{4}$ inches

FERGUSON—FISHERS ISLAND PLATE III

SPEAR POINTS AND SCRAPERS OF STONE

Length of *b*, 5 $\frac{9}{16}$ inches

FERGUSON—FISHERS ISLAND PLATE IV

STONE HOE BLADES

Length of *a*, 10$\frac{1}{2}$ inches

GROOVED STONE AXE-BLADES
Length of *c*, 9¾ inches

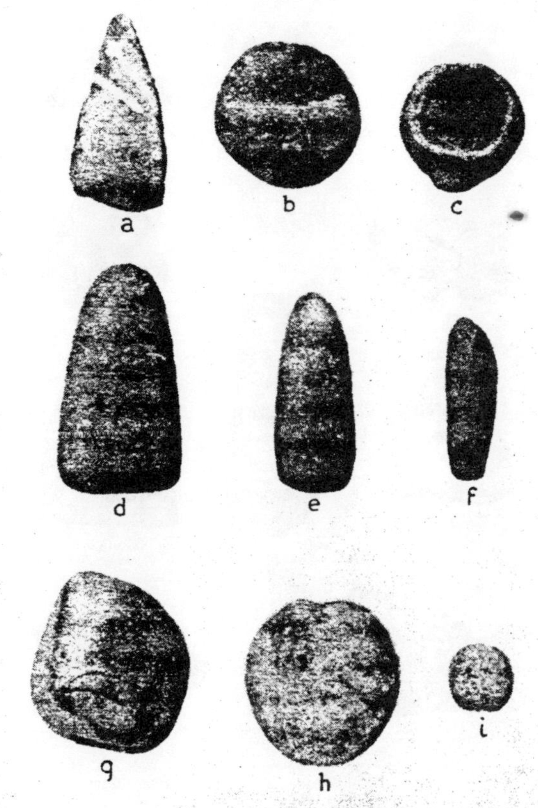

VARIOUS OBJECTS OF STONE
Length of *d*, 3⅝ inches

PESTLE, GRINDER AND NET SINKER OF STONE
Length of *a*, 10⅛ inches

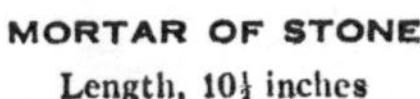

MORTAR OF STONE
Length, 10½ inches

FERGUSON—FISHERS ISLAND PLATE IX

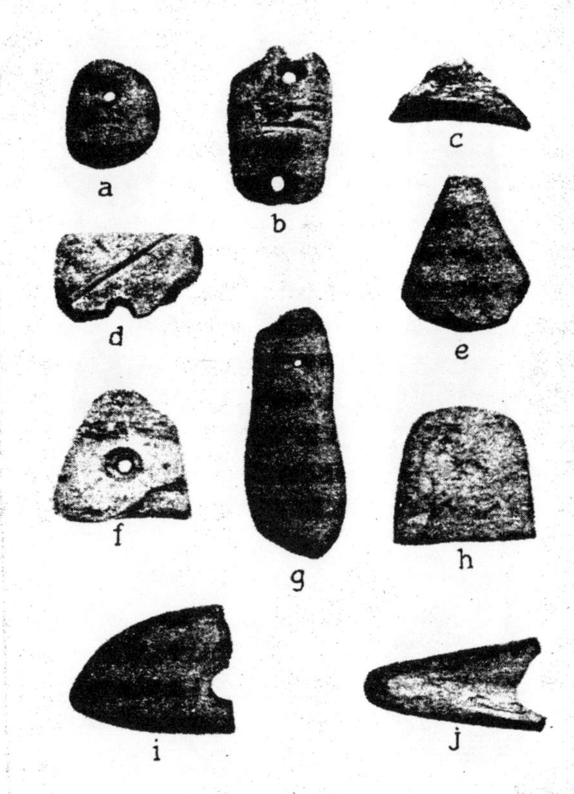

VARIOUS OBJECTS OF STONE
Length of *g*, 2 11/16 inches

FERGUSON—FISHERS ISLAND PLATE X

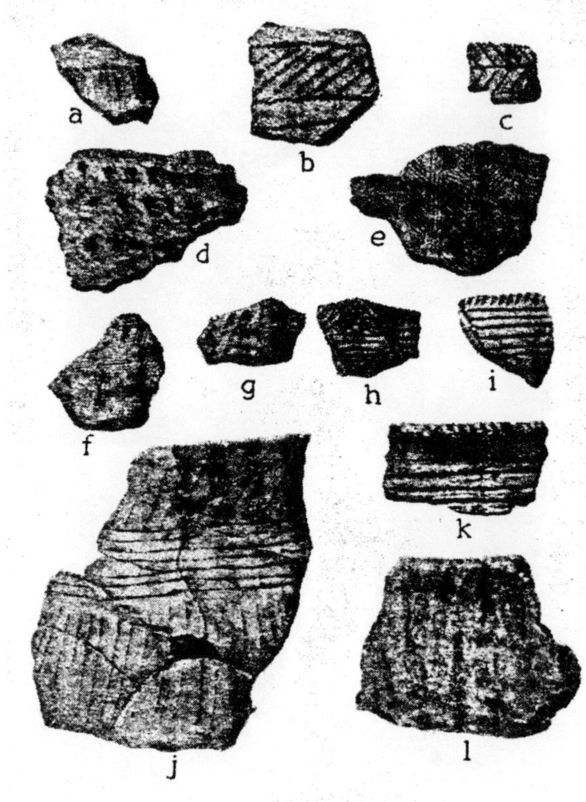

POTSHERDS
Height of *j*, 4½ inches

FERGUSON—FISHERS ISLAND PLATE XI

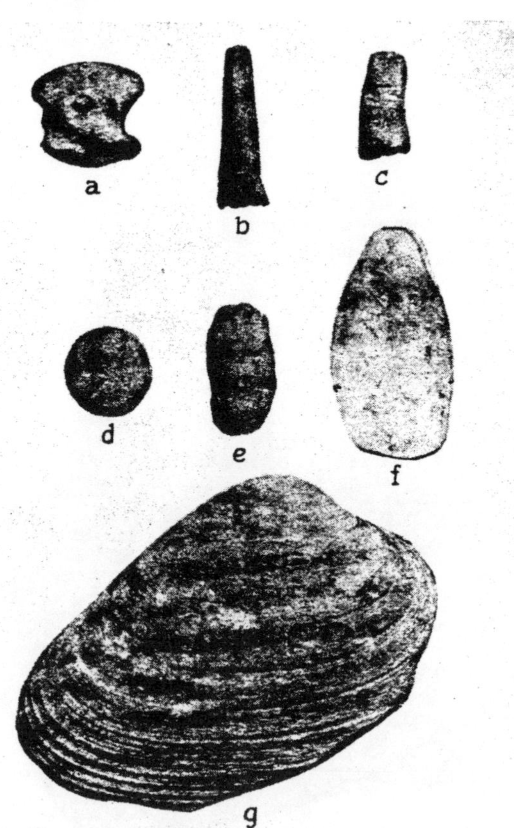

VARIOUS OBJECTS OF POTTERY AND SHELL
Length of *g*, 6 inches

FERGUSON—FISHERS ISLAND PLATE XII

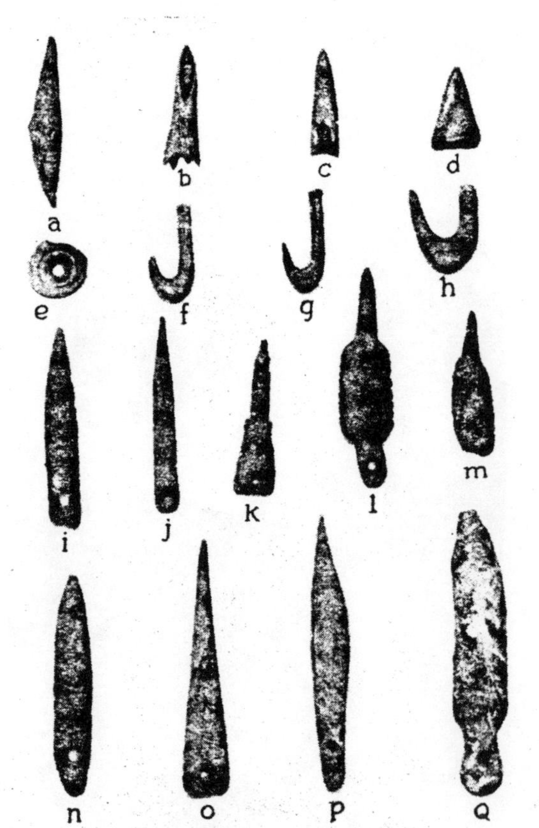

VARIOUS OBJECTS OF BONE
Length of *q*, 3¼ inches

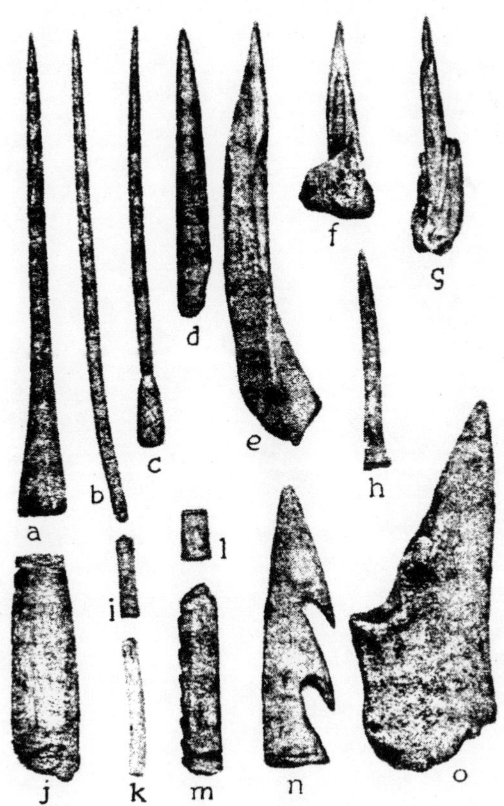

VARIOUS OBJECTS OF BONE
Length of *n*, 3½ inches